PETER SEREFINE

Trust Shattered

Cases of Government Betrayal

- A Beacon Of Common Sense -
www.Liberty-Lighthouse.com

"Every member of the State ought diligently to read and to study the constitution of his country, and teach the rising generation to be free. By knowing their rights, they will sooner perceive when they are violated and be the better prepared to defend and assert them."

John Jay, author of five of The Federalist Papers and the first Chief Justice of the United States.

Contents

Foreword   iv
Preface   viii

I Betrayed Bodies: Government's Unauthorized Human Trials

 1 Nuremberg Code (1947)   3
 2 Compulsory Sterilization (1907-1981)   7
 3 Tuskegee Syphilis Study (1932-1972)   10
 4 Guatemalan   Syphilis   Experiments
    (1946-1948)   13
 5 The Polio Vaccine (1955)   16
 6 Human Radiation Experiments (1940s-1970s)   19
 7 Project 112 (1962-1973)   22
 8 Project SHAD (1962-1973)   25
 9 San Francisco Biological Warfare Tests (1950s)   28
10 Operation Sea-Spray (1950)   31
11 Agent Orange Testing (1960s)   34
12 MKUltra (1950s-1960s)   37
13 Project Sunshine (1950s-1960s)   40
14 Project Big Buzz (1955)   43
15 Plum Island Animal Disease Center
    (1950s-1970s)   46
16 Operation Whitecoat (1954-1973)   49

17 Nutritional Guidelines and the Food Pyramid   52
18 FDA revocation   55
19 CoVid-19 (2020)   59
20 Part I Conclusion   62

II Betrayed Liberties: Government's Erosion of Freedom

21 The Alien and Sedition Acts (1798)   67
22 Japanese Internment during World War II   70
23 McCarthyism and the Red Scare (1950s)   74
24 COINTELPRO (1956-1971)   78
25 NSA Surveillance (ongoing)   82
26 Patriot Act (2001)   85
27 Censorship and Internet Regulation (ongoing)   89
28 Permission Society   93
29 Victimless Crimes   96
30 Right to Protest   100
31 COVID-19 Pandemic   103
32 January 6th, 2021   108
33 Part II Conclusion   114

III Betrayed Estates: Property's Conquest by Authority

34 Eminent Domain   119
35 Inflation   122
36 Gun Control Laws   126
37 Zoning and Land Use Regulations   129
38 Regulatory Takings   132
39 Property Tax   135

40 Rent Control   139
41 Environmental Regulations   144
42 Civil Asset Forfeiture   148
43 Income Tax   151
44 Inheritance Tax   154
45 Estate Tax   158
46 Consumer Product Bans   161
47 COVID-19 Lockdowns   165
48 Part III Conclusion   169

49 Conclusion   172
Epilogue   175
Nuremberg Code   177
About the Author   180
Also by Peter Serefine   182

Foreword

The mailman delivers!

Once again, Peter Serefine, mailman by day and American constitutionalist and historian by passion, has put together a book that is a must-read for any American who wants to "do better" at being an American. Trust Shattered gives a reader an opportunity to understand the present and prepare for the future by freeing and confronting the ghosts many would wish to keep hidden in America's attic.

Three decades ago, when I decided to convert from the Anglican faith to Roman Catholicism, it was not enough for me to simply through the required RCIA (Rite of Christian Initiation for Adults) process. I wanted to understand exactly what it meant to be Catholic and, almost more importantly, I wanted to understand the history of what it has meant to be Catholic over millennia. I joined up with the Jesuits and enrolled in the Catholic Studies program at Loyola University-Chicago.

My thinking was that if was going to be a practicing Catholic (a Christian faith denomination from which I have since departed) I needed to understand both the theology and the history. The need to understand the theology is apparent, but my need to understand the history was a bit less transparent to some. My thought was, if I was going to defend the church today and offer it up to someone else for tomorrow, I first had to know its past; warts and all. To simply brush it aside with a version of, "that was then, this is now" was too intellectually lazy for me.

Coming to learn the past of the Catholic Church, a mixture of miracles, courage, teaching, violence, debauchery, and persecution, made my time in the Church in the late 20th and early 21st Centuries reconcilable. Enlightenment eliminated denial. I could honestly say that I had looked at the excesses of Roman Catholicism, but I could still find a way to celebrate the virtue found in the sacraments.

This is exactly what Peter Serefine has given Americans the opportunity to do within the pages of Trust Shattered. This book will become a key back-packet reference book for every American to carry around and quickly turn to whenever they are confronted with an accusation that America isn't perfect. It isn't! No place on earth is. The question that should always be answered is: Having honestly examined our shortcomings, is this still a good place to be? Belligerence and blind-obedience is not a substitute for acknowledgment and acceptance of fault. Trust Shattered shows there is much fault to acknowledge and accept in America's history, especially when it comes to using people as pawns for various and nefarious gain by the ruling and profiteering classes.

Organized nicely by category, this book becomes the quick reference guide to virtually every valid conspiracy theory that has surfaced within our shores over 200-plus years. I use the words "valid" and "theory" quite deliberately. Today we produce conspiracy notions around virtually every news story in every cycle. This cheapens the fact that conspiracies really do exist and turns us into a nation of fools. If everything is a conspiracy, then nothing is. The plain truth is that conspiracies have and do exist and Serefine within these pages identifies all of the major ones that have been verified through time and testimony.

With regard to the word "theory," let me say that we misuse the term regularly. What we mostly have today are conspiracy hypotheses; things we have formed by observation, but which have not really been tested or proven. Serefine has put together a book of tested conspiracy hypotheses and shown that they are valid. By looking at these documented abuses form the past, we are able to explain the present and predict the future. That is the definition of a theory!

What one has to love about Peter Serefine, is that despite his thorough, methodical, and intelligent portrayal of America's "sins," he remains a man who loves this country and loves our Constitution. He has devoted his time, treasure, and talent to explaining it and defending it. Even this book, a chronicle of American abuses and transgressions, is a testament to his love for country. Far from trying to tear it down, he is attempting to shore it up by exposing its imperfections and then saying, without having to actually say, "we are still standing! Let's just do better!"

In the end, those who wish to destroy our country, those participating in this totalitarian-globalist movement, always want to point to America's imperfections as proof that it needs to be completely dismantled. To such arguments, I respond with the sentiment expressed by the late Catholic Priest and best-selling author, Father Andrew Greeley. In responding to those who wanted to throw out the Catholic Church along with the pedophilia-scandal bathwater, his reply was along the lines of:

If you wish to join the perfect church, seek it. When you find it, join it. Then know from that moment forward it will cease to be perfect.

Peter Serefine in this collection exposes and peels back America's imperfections so that we might see the beauty in that which is still worth saving. One way to contemplate constructive criticism is to say it is that which allows you to accentuate and improve upon the best of what remains outside of the critique. Peter leaves America standing; naked and shivering, but standing.

I tip my hat to the independent scholar who has done good work by placing so much work into shining a bright light on the evils and machinations of what free people have done to free people over the past 200 years. We are still, to a large extent, a free people. Let's see if we can do better.

Brent E. Hamachek
  Vice President & Assoc Publisher
  with Human Events Media Group

Preface

According to the Declaration of Independence, the purpose of government is to protect the unalienable rights of its citizens—rights to life, liberty, and the pursuit of happiness. Yet, as history has shown, the US government has repeatedly betrayed these sacred trusts.

In "Trust Shattered," I embark on a journey through the dark side of government power, exploring the ways in which the US government has infringed upon the lives, liberties, and property of its citizens. Through chilling accounts of clandestine human experimentation, relentless attacks on freedom, and the trampling of property rights, I challenge readers to reexamine the very essence of government's role in our lives.

"Trust Shattered" is divided into three thought-provoking sections based on the philosophical roots of John Locke's enduring concepts: life, liberty, and property.

Part 1: Betrayed Bodies: Government's Unauthorized Human Trials. The stories within these pages reveal the ways in which government institutions, once entrusted with safeguarding the well-being of their citizens, betrayed that sacred trust in the pursuit of their own agendas.

Part 2: Betrayed Liberties: Government's Erosion of Freedom. In this section, we embark on a historical and contemporary journey, unveiling instances where government actions have encroached upon the cherished ideal of liberty. We confront the disconcerting tension between authority and individual freedom.

Part 3: Betrayed Estates: Property's Conquest by Authority. As we continue our odyssey, we navigate the terrain of property rights. Here, we expose moments and methods when ownership and security have become vulnerable to the whims of governance, questioning the very dynamics that shape our rights to what we possess.

This book is not simply a historical account; it is also a call to action. In the face of government betrayal, we must demand accountability and transparency, and stand firm in defense of our unalienable rights. By delving into these narratives, I hope to empower individuals and communities to question, advocate for justice, and shape a brighter future.

As we embark on this journey through the shadows of betrayal, let us remember that within the darkness lies the potential for enlightenment. Within the narratives of betrayal lie the lessons that can pave the path toward a future where life, liberty, and property are safeguarded as the foundation of a just society.

I

Betrayed Bodies: Government's Unauthorized Human Trials

Part 1, "Betrayed Bodies: Government's Unauthorized Human Trials" examines the legacy of government betrayals in the realm of medical research. Through a careful examination of historical cases, the author demonstrates that government overreach in the realm of medical research can have devastating consequences for individuals and society as a whole.

1

Nuremberg Code (1947)

Historical Context

The Nuremberg Code was developed in the aftermath of World War II, in response to the horrific human experiments conducted by Nazi doctors on concentration camp inmates. These experiments were carried out without the consent of the participants, and they resulted in untold suffering and death.

After the war, the Allies put the Nazi doctors on trial for their crimes. The United States Army Medical Corps played a key role in the trials, and it was during this time that the Nuremberg Code was developed.

The Nuremberg Code is a set of 10 principles that govern the ethics of human experimentation. These principles include:

- Informed consent: Participants in experiments must

provide their voluntary and informed consent.
- Avoidance of unnecessary suffering: Experiments should not cause unnecessary physical or mental suffering.
- Potential benefits must outweigh the risks: The potential benefits of an experiment must outweigh the risks to the participants.
- The well-being of the participant is the primary concern: The well-being of the individual participant should always be the primary concern.

The Nuremberg Code was a landmark document in the history of medical ethics. It was the first international code of ethics to govern human experimentation, and it has had a profound impact on the way that medical research is conducted today, or did it?

The Shadows of Betrayal

The Nuremberg Code was intended to prevent the atrocities of Nazi human experimentation from ever happening again. However, as the chapters that follow will reveal, the Nuremberg Code was often ignored or violated in the years after its adoption.

> *"The great weight of the evidence before us to effect that certain types of medical experiments on human beings, when kept within reasonably well-defined bounds, conform to the ethics of the medical profession generally."*
> *— Nuremberg Code, 1947*

There are a number of factors that contributed to these

betrayals. One factor was the Cold War. The United States and the Soviet Union were engaged in a race to develop new military technologies, and they were willing to sacrifice human rights in order to achieve their goals.

"The failure to provide essential protections against the risks that arose from these experiments was, and remains today, a profound betrayal of the trust that we owe to our service members and to our veterans." — Advisory Committee on Human Radiation Experiments, 1995

Another factor that contributed to the violation of the Nuremberg Code was the secrecy that surrounded many government-funded research programs. These programs were often classified, and they were not subject to public scrutiny. This made it easier for researchers to get away with unethical practices.

Finally, the Nuremberg Code was often violated because of a lack of accountability. Researchers who conducted unethical experiments were rarely punished. This created a climate in which unethical practices were tolerated, if not encouraged.

The Legacy of the Nuremberg Code

The Nuremberg Code is a reminder that we must always be vigilant in protecting the rights of the vulnerable and that we must never sacrifice human dignity for the sake of scientific progress.

"The code was a product of its time, but it remains a powerful moral compass for all who conduct human

research today." — United States Department of Health & Human Services, 1996

The code's principles are as important today as they were when they were first drafted. We must continue to uphold these principles and to ensure that they are respected by all researchers, regardless of their nationality or the nature of their work.

Conclusion

The Nuremberg Code is a testament to the resilience of the human spirit. It was born out of the darkest pages of human history, yet it represents a commitment to ethical conduct and the protection of individual rights.

The shadows of betrayal that cast themselves over the Nuremberg Code's legacy remind us that the fight for ethical human experimentation is never over. We must continue to be vigilant and to speak out against all forms of unethical research.

By upholding the promise of the Nuremberg Code, we can honor the victims of past betrayals and build a better future for all.

2

Compulsory Sterilization (1907-1981)

The history of compulsory sterilization in the United States unveils a disturbing narrative of governmental overreach and ethical breaches in public health. This chapter delves into the emergence, execution, and eventual cessation of these programs, reflecting on their profound impact on thousands of lives.

Roots in Eugenic Ideology

The roots of compulsory sterilization lie in the early 20th century eugenics movement, a disturbing chapter in public health history. Misguided by the pursuit of genetic 'purity', eugenicists, twisting Darwinian principles, pushed for laws that mandated sterilization for those deemed genetically 'unfit'. Targeting individuals with mental illnesses, intellectual disabilities, and more, these laws were a gross misapplication of science, stemming from a flawed understanding of genetics and heredity.

Widespread and Discriminatory Practices

During this period, over 60,000 Americans, predominantly women, ethnic minorities, the impoverished, and the disabled, were forcibly sterilized. These actions represented a glaring violation of reproductive rights and human dignity, disproportionately affecting the most vulnerable and marginalized in society. The state-sanctioned sterilizations, often conducted without genuine informed consent and at times under the guise of other medical procedures, demonstrated a shocking disregard for individual autonomy and ethical medical practice.

Government Sanction and Supreme Court Endorsement

A significant moment in this history was the 1927 Supreme Court ruling in Buck v. Bell, where Justice Oliver Wendell Holmes Jr.'s infamous words, "Three generations of imbeciles are enough," endorsed the sterilization of Carrie Buck, a young woman unjustly labeled as 'feebleminded'. This ruling provided judicial sanction to these practices, catalyzing their spread across the nation. The last known forced sterilization occurred in 1981, highlighting the persistence of eugenic thinking in certain governmental policies, even after its scientific and ethical foundations had been discredited.

Seeking Justice and Reckoning with the Past

The aftermath of these sterilization programs led to efforts seeking justice for the victims, including legal actions, calls for reparations, and public acknowledgments of these human rights violations. These efforts underscore the continuous need for ethical oversight in government and healthcare practices.

Legacy and Contemporary Lessons

The legacy of this era serves as a crucial reminder of the dangers posed by pseudoscientific beliefs infiltrating policy and medical ethics. It underscores the importance of upholding individual rights, informed consent, and human dignity in healthcare and public policymaking. As we reflect on this dark chapter, it is imperative to advocate for reproductive rights and maintain vigilance against any form of coerced medical intervention, ensuring respect for personal autonomy and dignity.

3

Tuskegee Syphilis Study (1932-1972)

The Tuskegee Syphilis Study remains one of the most notorious examples of ethical misconduct in American medical history. Conducted between 1932 and 1972 in Tuskegee, Alabama, it involved the deliberate and deceitful non-treatment of syphilis in 600 African American men. This study represents a profound violation of human rights and a significant breach of trust within the medical system.

Historical Context

This study was set against a backdrop of systemic racism and discrimination in the United States. At a time when African Americans faced significant barriers to quality healthcare, the Tuskegee study exploited racial vulnerabilities. The limited contemporary understanding of syphilis and its effects played into the researchers' disregard for the severe risks to the participants.

Deception and Exploitation

In the Tuskegee study, researchers misled participants regarding their health, falsely claiming to treat "bad blood" – a term used at the time for various illnesses – while deliberately concealing their true diagnosis of syphilis. Even after penicillin became available as an effective treatment, the participants were deliberately denied access to it. Coercive tactics, including the provision of free healthcare and legal threats, were employed to ensure continued participation.

Ethical Violations and Impact

The study continued decades past the establishment of the Nuremberg Code, violating its central tenets:

- **Informed Consent:** Participants were not truthfully informed about the study's nature and the associated risks.
- **Autonomy:** The men's right to make informed decisions about their healthcare was systematically denied.
- **Nonmaleficence:** Researchers failed to prevent harm to the participants.
- **Justice:** The selection of participants was racially motivated, not based on medical need.

The ramifications of this study were catastrophic. Many participants suffered severe health complications, and the disease was even passed on to some of their partners. Furthermore, the study severely damaged the trust between the African-American community and healthcare providers, a legacy that persists to this day.

Lessons Learned and Upholding Ethical Principles

The Tuskegee Syphilis Study serves as a grim reminder of the critical importance of ethics in medical research. It highlights the need for informed consent, respect for patient autonomy, and the moral duty of researchers to protect their subjects. To prevent a recurrence of such atrocities, it is essential to commit unwaveringly to ethical principles in all medical research. This commitment involves ensuring comprehensive informed consent, respecting the rights and dignity of research participants, and actively working to rebuild trust between the medical community and minority groups, particularly those historically exploited by the healthcare system.

Conclusion

The Tuskegee Syphilis Study stands as a cautionary tale about the perils of disregarding human rights in medical research. It underscores the imperative to protect vulnerable populations from exploitation and to maintain the highest ethical standards in all scientific endeavors. Remembering and learning from this dark chapter in history is crucial in our collective effort to ensure that such violations of human dignity are never repeated.

4

Guatemalan Syphilis Experiments (1946-1948)

The Guatemalan Syphilis Experiments, conducted between 1946 and 1948, stand as a stark example of the ethical transgressions of governmental medical research beyond national boundaries. Targeting non-U.S. citizens, these experiments epitomize a disturbing era where human rights were overshadowed by the pursuit of scientific knowledge.

Global Reach of Unethical Research

Under the aegis of the U.S. Public Health Service and spearheaded by Dr. John C. Cutler, approximately 1,500 Guatemalan individuals, including soldiers, prisoners, and psychiatric patients, were deliberately infected with syphilis and other sexually transmitted diseases. The selection of these non-U.S. citizens and the setting in Guatemala reflect a grave ethical disregard for certain populations, considered less deserving of ethical protections due to their nationality and social status.

Violation of Universal Ethical Principles

The primary ethical violation in these experiments lay in the lack of informed consent and the intentional deception of the participants. These individuals, vulnerable and marginalized, were exploited in the name of scientific progress, a blatant contravention of universal ethical standards which should transcend geographical and national boundaries.

Impact and Accountability

The aftermath of these experiments was tragic, with at least 83 deaths and numerous others suffering from the effects of untreated syphilis. The disclosure of these experiments in 2010 led to global outrage and subsequent apologies from U.S. President Barack Obama, Secretary of State Hillary Clinton, and Secretary of Health and Human Services Kathleen Sebelius, reflecting an acknowledgment of the grievous ethical breaches committed.

Implications for International Research Ethics

The Guatemalan Syphilis Experiments underscore the critical need for robust ethical oversight in international medical research. These events have played a pivotal role in strengthening ethical standards globally, emphasizing the importance of informed consent, respect for human dignity, and the protection of vulnerable populations in all medical research endeavors.

Conclusion

The Guatemalan Syphilis Experiments serve as a sobering reminder of the imperative to maintain ethical integrity in medical research, irrespective of the nationality of the subjects. This episode in history urges us to prioritize human rights and dignity above scientific exploration and to recognize the universal applicability of ethical principles in all research, highlighting the responsibility to protect all individuals from such exploitation.

5

The Polio Vaccine (1955)

T he development of the polio vaccine marks a pivotal moment in medical history, symbolizing both a monumental scientific achievement and a complex ethical quandary. This chapter explores the intricate narrative of the polio vaccine, highlighting the triumph over polio and the ethical and safety concerns that cast a shadow over this landmark discovery.

The Triumph Against Polio

In the early 20th century, polio emerged as a formidable health menace, leading to widespread fear and suffering. The introduction of Dr. Jonas Salk's polio vaccine in 1955 was celebrated as a major medical breakthrough, offering hope to eradicate a disease that had plagued humanity for generations. However, this path to victory was not without its ethical quandaries and safety missteps.

Ethical and Safety Issues

- **Contamination and the Cutter Incident:** A significant setback occurred in 1955 with the Cutter Incident, where a manufacturing error by Cutter Laboratories resulted in vaccines containing live poliovirus. This led to over 250 cases of induced polio, causing paralysis and fatalities and significantly undermining public confidence in vaccines.
- **Ethical Concerns in Vaccine Trials:** The polio vaccine's development was marred by ethical issues, notably in its testing phase. Human subjects, including children, were used in trials without adequate consent, highlighting a disregard for individual rights and medical ethics.
- **The SV40 Controversy:** Further complicating the vaccine's legacy was the discovery of Simian Virus 40 (SV40) contamination in some vaccine batches. Though the link between SV40 and cancer remains inconclusive, this raised serious concerns about vaccine safety and production standards.

Impact on Public Trust

The controversies and setbacks in the development and deployment of the polio vaccine had lasting implications for public trust in medical institutions and government oversight. The Cutter Incident, in particular, catalyzed reforms in vaccine production and regulatory processes. However, restoring public confidence in vaccines and health authorities proved to be a more prolonged and challenging endeavor.

Conclusion

The narrative of the polio vaccine encapsulates the dual aspects of scientific success and ethical responsibility. It underscores the need for rigorous safety standards and ethical considerations in medical research and vaccine development. Reflecting on this chapter in medical history, we are reminded of the critical importance of maintaining public trust, balancing the advancement of medical science with the protection of individual rights, and upholding the principles of ethical healthcare.

6

Human Radiation Experiments (1940s-1970s)

In a troubling chapter of the 20th century, the United States government conducted a series of covert human radiation experiments. These experiments, spanning from the 1940s through the 1970s, are a stark reminder of the potential for ethical violations in the pursuit of scientific knowledge. This chapter explores these experiments and their implications, uncovering the uncomfortable truths of government betrayal and ethical transgressions.

The Quest for Knowledge, the Cost of Betrayal

During the Cold War era, the urgency to understand the effects of radiation on the human body led scientists down a path marred by ethical compromises. The government's pursuit of knowledge came at the expense of the human rights of countless individuals who were subjected to radiation without their consent or knowledge.

Unknowing Subjects in Ethical Quandaries

Central to the ethical breach of these experiments was the use of unknowing subjects, including prisoners, military personnel, and hospital patients. These individuals were exposed to radiation without informed consent, violating the core principles of autonomy and respect for persons. Among the most harrowing of these experiments was the exposure of pregnant women to radiation, under the guise of medical research, without disclosing the true risks involved.

Legacy of Suffering and Ethical Reckoning

The human radiation experiments left a legacy of physical and psychological suffering. The health impacts, including cancer and other serious illnesses, were profound and long-lasting. This period in scientific research raised fundamental questions about the morality of sacrificing individual well-being for the sake of knowledge and highlighted the need for strict ethical oversight in scientific endeavors.

The Price of Unchecked Power

These experiments reflect a disturbing chapter where the quest for scientific and military superiority overshadowed ethical considerations. They serve as a cautionary tale about the dangers of unchecked government power in scientific research. The story compels us to reflect on the balance between scientific advancement and moral responsibility, emphasizing the critical need for transparency and the protection of individual rights.

Lessons in Accountability

The revelations of these human radiation experiments have fundamentally shaped our understanding of ethical research practices. They underscore the importance of informed consent, transparency, and accountability in all scientific endeavors. This history teaches us the value of vigilance in safeguarding human dignity and autonomy, particularly in government-sponsored research.

Conclusion

The legacy of the human radiation experiments is a somber reminder of the ethical complexities inherent in scientific exploration. It highlights the imperative to prioritize human rights and ethical standards above scientific inquiry. As we move forward, it is essential to remember this chapter of history, not only as a reflection of past failings but as a guidepost for ethical and responsible research in the future.

7

Project 112 (1962-1973)

The narrative of Project 112, active from 1962 to 1973, serves as a stark reminder of the potential consequences when government overreach infringes upon the constitutional rights of individuals. This project, involving undisclosed exposure of military personnel to hazardous agents, stands as a blatant violation of the principles of life, liberty, and property enshrined in the United States Constitution.

Unveiling Project 112's Hidden Agenda

Initiated under the pretense of enhancing military preparedness, Project 112's real aim was to develop and test chemical and biological weapons. Conducted in secrecy, this project symbolizes a grave betrayal of trust, as personnel were neither informed about the true nature of the experiments nor given a chance to consent. This lack of transparency and deception not only breached ethical standards but also contravened the fundamental values of individual autonomy and liberty.

An Ethical Breach of Trust

The project treated military personnel as unwitting participants in hazardous experiments, exposing them to serious risks without their knowledge. This ethical breach was compounded by the secrecy surrounding the project, obstructing the participants' ability to make informed decisions and challenging the accountability of those responsible.

The Toll on Health and Trust

The repercussions of Project 112 were profound, extending beyond immediate health risks. Participants suffered various health issues, from respiratory problems to cancer, alongside psychological impacts like anxiety, depression, and PTSD. More broadly, this betrayal eroded their trust in the government and compromised their sense of duty, reflecting a deep-seated impact on their lives and well-being.

The Imperative of Upholding Constitutional Rights

Project 112 starkly illustrates the necessity of government accountability and adherence to constitutional rights. It underscores the duty of government officials to uphold the rights of all individuals, as mandated by the Constitution. The project's legacy is a reminder of the obligation of those in power to adhere to the highest ethical standards and the oath to protect the Constitution.

Learning from the Shadows of History

Project 112 is a somber chapter in American history, highlighting the dangers of government overreach and the crucial importance of safeguarding fundamental rights. It teaches us the value of accountability, transparency, and the unwavering protection of individual liberties. As we reflect on this episode, it becomes clear that remembering and learning from such betrayals is essential to prevent their recurrence and to ensure that the principles of the Constitution are upheld.

8

Project SHAD (1962-1973)

Project SHAD (Shipboard Hazard and Defense), a subset of the controversial Project 112, represents a significant ethical dilemma in the history of U.S. military experiments. Conducted during the 1960s, this project violated the constitutional rights of military personnel by exposing them to chemical and biological agents without informed consent. This chapter explores the ethical breaches and the lasting impact of Project SHAD, underlining the necessity of transparency and accountability in government actions.

The Secrecy of Project 112 and SHAD

Project SHAD, an extension of Project 112, was aimed at assessing shipboard vulnerability to chemical and biological warfare. Conducted in utmost secrecy, these experiments were emblematic of the government's prioritization of military preparedness over individual rights. The lack of transparency and informed consent in these projects highlights a profound betrayal of trust among military personnel, who were unknowingly subjected to potential health hazards.

Violations of Informed Consent

Central to the ethical violations in Project SHAD was the disregard for the principle of informed consent. Military personnel, serving as human subjects, were not given complete information about the experiments, nor were they provided an opportunity to opt out. This failure to obtain voluntary and informed consent goes against the core tenets of ethical research, demonstrating a grave disrespect for the autonomy and well-being of the participants.

The Unraveling of Secrecy and Impact on Individuals

The secrecy surrounding Project SHAD and its parent project, Project 112, persisted for decades until veterans began to voice health concerns in the late 1990s. This led to a gradual disclosure of information, although incomplete and redacted. The physical and psychological toll on participants, including illnesses like cancer and respiratory problems, as well as feelings of betrayal and mistrust, reflect the deep-seated impact of these experiments.

Ethical Imperatives Ignored and the Call for Accountability

Project SHAD, alongside Project 112, starkly illustrates the consequences of ethical neglect in government-led research. The blatant disregard for fundamental ethical principles, such as informed consent and the right to autonomy, raises critical questions about the moral compass guiding such operations. The veterans who suffered due to these experiments represent a group wronged by their own government, deserving of recognition, justice, and compensation for their involuntary sacrifices.

Lessons from Project SHAD

Project SHAD serves as a sobering reminder of the importance of ethical conduct in government operations, especially those involving the military. It underscores the need for rigorous adherence to constitutional rights, transparent communication, and the safeguarding of individual liberties. As we reflect on this dark chapter, we are reminded of the paramount importance of holding governmental and military institutions accountable for their actions. Ensuring that such breaches of trust and ethical standards are not repeated is essential for maintaining the integrity of the military and the trust of those who serve.

9

San Francisco Biological Warfare Tests (1950s)

In the 1950s, against the tense backdrop of the Cold War, the U.S. government conducted covert biological warfare tests in San Francisco, marking a significant ethical breach in its duty to protect its citizens. This chapter examines the secretive nature of these tests, the ethical considerations overlooked, and the lasting impact on public trust and individual well-being.

The Veiled Experimentation

Amid heightened geopolitical tensions, the U.S. military initiated clandestine biological warfare tests, releasing bacteria over San Francisco to simulate the spread of biological agents in urban environments. The use of Serratia marcescens, Bacillus globigii, and Bacillus subtilis, under the guise of scientific research, constituted a gross violation of ethical norms and public trust.

Unwitting Citizens as Subjects

The most profound betrayal in these tests was the use of the city's inhabitants as unsuspecting test subjects. Without their knowledge or consent, nearly three-quarters of a million people were exposed to potentially harmful bacteria. This disregard for informed consent and the health risks imposed on the public highlights a troubling disregard for individual autonomy and safety.

A Fragile Trust Shattered

The revelation of these tests not only raised concerns about potential health effects but also significantly eroded public trust in the government. The citizens of San Francisco, who unknowingly became part of a hazardous experiment, experienced a profound betrayal that reverberated beyond the immediate health implications, damaging the relationship between the government and the governed.

Ethical Contemplation and Implications

The San Francisco Biological Warfare Tests compel us to confront the ethical dilemmas inherent in balancing scientific experimentation with national security interests. They highlight the critical importance of ethical considerations in government actions and the necessity of safeguarding individual rights against the excesses of state power. This incident serves as a cautionary tale, illustrating the dangerous consequences of prioritizing national security objectives over the principles of transparency, informed consent, and public welfare.

Lessons in Accountability

In the aftermath of these tests, the need for accountability and ethical governance became starkly evident. The story of the San Francisco tests teaches us the value of holding government and military institutions to account for their actions. It underscores the imperative of maintaining ethical standards in all government endeavors, particularly those that have the potential to impact public health and safety.

Conclusion

The legacy of the San Francisco Biological Warfare Tests is a reminder of the delicate balance between scientific inquiry, national security, and ethical responsibility. As we reflect on this chapter in history, it is clear that the protection of citizen rights, adherence to ethical standards, and the cultivation of public trust are essential components of a just and free society. Acknowledging and learning from the mistakes of the past is crucial in ensuring that such violations of trust and ethics are not repeated in the future.

10

Operation Sea-Spray (1950)

Operation Sea-Spray, conducted in 1950, stands as a significant event in the history of government secrecy and ethical controversy. This covert operation by the U.S. Navy, involving the release of Serratia marcescens bacteria over San Francisco, highlights a profound breach of trust between the government and its citizens. This chapter explores the operation's objectives, ethical transgressions, and the long-term implications for public trust and policy.

Unearthing the Secrets of Operation Sea-Spray

As part of a broader series of biological warfare tests, Operation Sea-Spray was intended to assess the dispersion and impact of biological agents in a populated area. The use of Serratia marcescens, typically harmless but with potential health risks, in an unsuspecting urban environment, underscores the ethical quandaries faced by military and government institutions in the pursuit of national security.

Betrayal of Trust and Informed Consent

Central to the ethical dilemma of Operation Sea-Spray was the absence of informed consent. The citizens of San Francisco, unknowingly exposed to a biological agent, were deprived of their right to make informed decisions about their participation. This action not only violated the Nuremberg Code's principles but also eroded the foundational trust necessary between a government and its people.

Ethical Implications and Unintended Consequences

The immediate physical health risks of Operation Sea-Spray, while significant, were overshadowed by the broader ethical implications and the psychological impact on the city's residents. The revelation of their involuntary involvement in such an experiment led to a deep-seated mistrust in government actions, highlighting the need for transparency and accountability in governmental research.

Learning from History's Lessons

The legacy of Operation Sea-Spray serves as a critical lesson in the ethics of scientific experimentation and governmental responsibility. It emphasizes the necessity of adhering to ethical standards, such as informed consent and transparency, to prevent the erosion of public trust and to safeguard the well-being of citizens.

Upholding Ethical Principles

Operation Sea-Spray's narrative is a compelling call to uphold ethical principles in all forms of research and governance. Recognizing the importance of individual rights, informed consent, and governmental accountability is imperative in forging a future where scientific endeavors are conducted with the highest ethical standards, ensuring the protection of life, dignity, and the rights of all individuals.

11

Agent Orange Testing (1960s)

The 1960s, a period marked by political and social upheaval, also witnessed a grave chapter of government betrayal: the testing and deployment of Agent Orange. This narrative sheds light on the harmful effects of this potent herbicide used in the Vietnam War, revealing the depth of its impact on both veterans and civilians and the long-lasting repercussions that continue to resonate.

The Tactical Use and Unintended Consequences

Agent Orange, primarily used to defoliate jungle cover in Vietnam, contained dioxin, a highly toxic compound. Initially employed as a military strategy to counter the Viet Cong, the broader implications of its use were vastly underestimated. The repercussions of Agent Orange exposure were far-reaching, affecting not only the immediate environment but also countless individuals, both Vietnamese and American.

Unsuspecting Test Subjects

The most significant betrayal in the Agent Orange saga was the exposure of soldiers and civilians to its toxic effects without informed consent. The lack of transparency regarding the health risks associated with Agent Orange exposure led to widespread, unintended harm. Both U.S. military personnel and Vietnamese civilians, unknowingly and without consent, became participants in what essentially amounted to a large-scale, uncontrolled chemical experiment.

The Devastating Fallout

The aftermath of Agent Orange exposure is a tapestry of physical and emotional suffering. Individuals exposed to the chemical suffered from various health problems, including cancers, respiratory issues, severe skin conditions, and the tragic occurrence of birth defects in subsequent generations. The anguish was not confined to the battlegrounds of Vietnam; returning U.S. veterans faced a healthcare system and government that were slow to acknowledge and address their plight.

The Betrayal Multiplied

The Agent Orange testing represents a twofold betrayal: the irresponsible use of a hazardous chemical without full comprehension of its long-term effects, and the subsequent failure of the government to adequately acknowledge and support the affected individuals. This neglect deepened the sense of betrayal among veterans and civilians, who struggled for recognition and justice amidst bureaucracy and indifference.

The Ongoing Struggle for Justice

The legacy of Agent Orange is a poignant reminder of the ethical responsibilities that accompany military strategies and scientific experimentation. It underscores the necessity for transparency, accountability, and the protection of human rights in government actions. As we acknowledge this painful chapter, we recognize the continuous struggle for justice and proper recognition faced by the victims. Honoring their sacrifices means committing to ethical integrity, transparency, and ensuring that such tragic mistakes are never repeated.

12

MKUltra (1950s-1960s)

The MKUltra project, spanning the 1950s and 1960s, stands as a chilling testament to the lengths government institutions may go in the pursuit of intelligence and military dominance. This clandestine operation, conducted by the CIA, delved into unethical mind control experiments, starkly illustrating the dangers of unchecked governmental power and the critical importance of ethical standards in scientific exploration.

The Veiled Agenda of MKUltra

MKUltra emerged from the shadows of the Cold War, driven by the CIA's quest to develop techniques for mind control and psychological manipulation. The project encompassed a wide range of experiments, from drug administration (like LSD) to sensory deprivation and psychological stress, all aimed at mastering the art of mental influence. Shrouded in secrecy, the operation's true extent and objectives were concealed from public scrutiny, leading to significant ethical breaches.

Exploiting Vulnerable Individuals

Central to MKUltra's controversy was the exploitation of vulnerable individuals, including prisoners, mental health patients, and uninformed citizens. These individuals were subjected to invasive and often damaging experiments without their consent, violating fundamental principles of human rights and dignity. The disregard for informed consent and autonomy in these experiments marked a profound betrayal of trust and ethical responsibility.

Ethical Crossroads and Betrayal of Trust

MKUltra's ethical violations are multifaceted, extending from the lack of transparency to the abandonment of informed consent and the protection of individual rights. The project not only infringed on the autonomy and well-being of its subjects but also eroded public trust in government institutions. The revelation of these experiments fueled a broader societal reckoning with the ethical boundaries of government-sanctioned research.

Legacy and the Balance of Power and Responsibility

The MKUltra project compels a deep reflection on the balance between governmental power and ethical responsibility. It highlights the potential for abuse when scientific inquiry is divorced from moral considerations and underscores the necessity of upholding ethical principles in all forms of research and governance.

Upholding Ethical Principles and Protecting Liberty

The legacy of MKUltra reinforces the imperative to uphold the Constitution and its immutable principles that safeguard the rights of all citizens. This episode in history serves as a cautionary tale about the potential consequences of government overreach and the importance of maintaining vigilance against any encroachments on individual liberties. As we move forward, it is crucial to remember and apply the lessons of MKUltra, ensuring that the pursuit of knowledge and security never again comes at the expense of fundamental human rights and ethical standards. By steadfastly adhering to the principles enshrined in the Constitution, we can prevent the recurrence of such transgressions and preserve the liberties that are the cornerstone of our free society.

13

Project Sunshine (1950s-1960s)

Project Sunshine, an obscure yet significant chapter within the broader context of MKUltra, represents a period marked by profound ethical transgressions in the name of scientific inquiry. In the 1950s and 1960s, this subproject embarked on an endeavor to understand the impact of nuclear fallout, crossing moral boundaries in its methods and approach. This chapter explores the inception, scope, and disturbing implications of Project Sunshine, particularly in relation to informed consent and individual rights.

The Unveiling of Project Sunshine

Project Sunshine's primary goal was to analyze the distribution of radioactive isotopes in human tissues to assess nuclear fallout's health effects. This objective, while scientifically grounded, was pursued through ethically questionable means. Tissue samples were collected from deceased individuals, including infants, without the consent of their families, leading to a covert operation fraught with moral implications.

Project Sunshine and the Web of Secrecy

Embedded within the larger framework of MKUltra, Project Sunshine's activities were interwoven with the project's overarching goals of mind control and psychological manipulation. This connection highlights the complex web of covert operations conducted by government agencies during this era, often blurring ethical lines and prioritizing strategic objectives over individual rights and autonomy.

Informed Consent and Individual Autonomy

The core ethical dilemma of Project Sunshine revolved around the absence of informed consent and the use of deception in procuring human tissue samples. The families of the deceased were unknowingly drawn into this experiment, highlighting a significant breach of ethical standards and the erosion of individual autonomy. This violation raises critical questions about the balance between scientific advancement and ethical conduct.

A Tarnished Pursuit of Knowledge

Project Sunshine's legacy is a troubling testament to the lengths government institutions have historically gone in the pursuit of knowledge. It compels us to reflect on the ethical responsibilities that accompany scientific research, especially when it intersects with human rights and individual dignity.

Guiding Principles for the Future

As we grapple with the historical implications of Project Sunshine, we are reminded of the paramount importance of adhering to ethical principles such as informed consent, transparency, and respect for individual rights. Recognizing the missteps of the past is crucial in forging a path forward that is characterized by responsible research, ethical integrity, and an unwavering commitment to protecting life, dignity, and autonomy. The lessons from Project Sunshine serve as a guiding beacon for future scientific endeavors, ensuring that the pursuit of knowledge is always aligned with the highest ethical standards.

14

Project Big Buzz (1955)

Project Big Buzz, unfolding in 1955, represents a controversial chapter in the annals of government experimentation. This covert project, aimed at exploring the use of mosquitoes as vectors for biological warfare, reflects the complex interplay between national security concerns and ethical considerations. This chapter examines the motivations behind the project, its ethical and environmental implications, and the lasting impact on public trust and environmental stewardship.

Unveiling the Project's Origins

Initiated amidst the pervasive atmosphere of the Cold War, Project Big Buzz was driven by the strategic goal of leveraging disease-carrying mosquitoes as potential biological weapons. The project involved releasing thousands of mosquitoes to understand their dispersal and potential use in warfare. While framed within the context of national defense, the initiative opened a Pandora's box of ethical and ecological concerns.

The Unintended Outcomes

The implementation of Project Big Buzz inadvertently fostered fear and anxiety among the public. The release of mosquitoes, although uninfected, ignited apprehensions about disease outbreaks, undermining public trust in government initiatives. This fear, born out of the lack of transparency and communication, highlights the broader ramifications of government experiments on public perception and trust.

Unraveling Ecosystems

Project Big Buzz's environmental consequences were profound. The mass release of mosquitoes had the potential to disrupt local ecosystems and alter ecological balances. This aspect of the project underscores the critical need to consider environmental impacts in the planning and execution of scientific and military endeavors.

Oversight and Accountability

The project's execution without public knowledge or consent raised significant ethical questions. It underscored the necessity of ethical oversight and government accountability in experimental practices. The project's secretive nature and potential risks to public health and the environment reflect a precarious balance between national security and ethical conduct.

Lessons from History

Project Big Buzz serves as a crucial historical lesson on the ethical complexities and unintended consequences of government experimentation. It prompts a reflection on the need for transparency, informed consent, and ethical decision-making in government projects, particularly those with potential public health and environmental impacts.

Navigating the Nexus of Ethics and Security

In retrospect, Project Big Buzz offers valuable insights into navigating the nexus between scientific exploration, national security, and ethical responsibility. It underscores the importance of prioritizing public trust, environmental stewardship, and ethical principles in government actions. Recognizing and learning from the project's missteps is essential in guiding future endeavors towards more responsible, transparent, and ethically sound practices.

15

Plum Island Animal Disease Center (1950s-1970s)

P lum Island Animal Disease Center, nestled in New York's Long Island Sound, presents a complex narrative of scientific pursuit interspersed with ethical quandaries. From the 1950s to the 1970s, the center was a focal point for animal disease research, encapsulating the tension between scientific progress and ethical responsibility. This chapter explores the center's operations, highlighting the challenges of maintaining transparency, ensuring informed consent, and balancing scientific advancement with ethical accountability.

The Enigmatic Island of Research

Established ostensibly to safeguard agriculture and public health from animal diseases, Plum Island harbored a more nuanced story. The center's research, while vital in preventing disease outbreaks, involved experiments on animals with diseases hazardous to both fauna and humans. The veil of secrecy around these operations brought to the fore critical discussions about the ethical dimensions of government-sponsored research.

Experiments on Animals

Central to Plum Island's narrative is the moral dilemma inherent in animal experimentation. The center's research practices, often resulting in animal suffering, posed significant ethical questions. The scientific community's responsibility to balance curiosity with compassion for living beings became a point of contention, underscoring the need for ethical guidelines in animal research.

Unintended Outcomes Beyond Animal Welfare

The repercussions of Plum Island's research extended beyond animal welfare, encompassing public health concerns and ecological implications. The possibility of zoonotic disease transmission highlighted the risks associated with such research, emphasizing the need for a comprehensive approach that considers the interdependence of ecosystems and human health.

A Call for Ethical Responsibility

The legacy of Plum Island Animal Disease Center serves as a crucial reminder of the ethical responsibilities incumbent upon scientific research, especially within government institutions. It underscores the importance of conducting research with a commitment to ethical principles, transparency, and respect for all life forms.

Navigating Ethical Imperatives in Scientific Research

As we reflect on the history of Plum Island, we are compelled to reexamine how government-sponsored research aligns with ethical imperatives. Ensuring that the pursuit of scientific knowledge adheres to standards of transparency, informed consent, and ethical conduct is paramount. The story of Plum Island challenges us to forge a path where scientific exploration and ethical responsibility coexist, safeguarding the dignity and rights of all living beings.

16

Operation Whitecoat (1954-1973)

O peration Whitecoat stands as a poignant example of the ethical complexities inherent in medical research, particularly under the pressures of the Cold War. This operation, involving conscientious objectors as subjects in medical experiments, brings to the forefront the intricate balance between the duty to serve, the protection of individual rights, and the quest for scientific knowledge. This chapter delves into the motivations, ethical considerations, and the lasting implications of this unique operation.

Conscientious Objectors and Unprecedented Service

Initiated in 1954, Operation Whitecoat was a response to the looming threat of biological warfare. Over 2,300 conscientious objectors, who opposed military service on moral or religious grounds, were recruited to participate in research that aimed to understand the effects of biological agents. This initiative raised profound ethical questions about the role of individual voluntarism in scientific experimentation during times of national crisis.

Informed Consent and Voluntarism

A pivotal ethical aspect of Operation Whitecoat was the principle of informed consent. Conscientious objectors volunteered for experiments that often involved exposure to disease-causing agents and unlicensed medical interventions. The ethical challenge lay in ensuring that these volunteers were fully aware of the potential risks, underscoring the importance of informed consent in medical research.

Navigating Ethical Tightropes

The participation of conscientious objectors in potentially harmful experiments highlights the delicate ethical balance in medical research. While their involvement was voluntary, the potential for harm raised significant ethical concerns, particularly regarding the principle of "primum non nocere" – first, do no harm. This principle, juxtaposed with the pursuit of critical scientific knowledge, epitomizes the moral dilemmas faced by researchers and participants alike.

Scientific Progress and Ethical Accountability

The legacy of Operation Whitecoat extends beyond its scientific contributions to biological research. It serves as a profound reminder of the ethical responsibilities that accompany scientific inquiry. The operation underscores the need for stringent ethical standards in medical research, particularly when it involves human subjects.

Striking a Delicate Balance

Reflecting on Operation Whitecoat, we are reminded of the continuous need to balance scientific advancement with ethical integrity. The conscientious objectors who participated in this operation navigated a complex ethical landscape, contributing to our understanding of biological agents while highlighting the paramount importance of protecting individual rights. As we move forward, Operation Whitecoat stands as a testament to the need for ongoing ethical vigilance in medical research, ensuring that the pursuit of knowledge always aligns with the highest standards of human dignity and respect.

17

Nutritional Guidelines and the Food Pyramid

The history of America's nutritional guidelines, epitomized by the Food Pyramid, presents a complex narrative where science, politics, and economics converge. This chapter explores the controversial evolution of these guidelines, shedding light on the interplay between shifting scientific consensus, industry influence, and public mistrust in the realm of healthy eating.

The Birth of the Food Pyramid

Introduced in 1992 by the USDA, the Food Pyramid was designed as a straightforward guide for a balanced diet. Its structure, emphasizing a grain-heavy diet with moderate consumption of meats and dairy and minimal fats and sweets, was initially hailed as a tool for healthy living. However, the foundational science and the influence of external funding soon became points of contention.

Shifting Scientific Paradigm

Nutritional science, the bedrock of the Food Pyramid, underwent significant transformations over time. Early endorsements of carbohydrate-rich, low-fat diets came under scrutiny with new research highlighting the complexities of dietary fats and the risks associated with high carbohydrate intake. These developments cast doubt on the Pyramid's reliability and its role in public health trends, particularly the increasing rates of obesity and diabetes.

Influence of the Food Industry

The integrity of the nutritional guidelines was further questioned upon revelations of the food industry's influence. Investigations pointed to substantial funding from grain and sugar manufacturers in the research behind the Pyramid, raising concerns about the potential prioritization of economic interests over scientific accuracy.

The Emergence of MyPlate

In response to criticism and evolving scientific insights, the USDA introduced MyPlate in 2011, replacing the Food Pyramid. While this new model sought to address earlier imbalances, skepticism persisted regarding industry influence and the overall effectiveness of the guidelines.

Public Health Implications

The impact of the Food Pyramid on public health has been significant. Critics argue that its high carbohydrate, low-fat emphasis contributed to widespread health issues like obesity and metabolic diseases. Additionally, the one-size-fits-all approach neglected individual dietary needs, potentially leading to inappropriate nutritional strategies for diverse populations.

The Crisis of Public Trust

The controversies surrounding the Food Pyramid and subsequent guidelines have led to a crisis of public trust in governmental nutritional advice. This situation has highlighted the necessity for more transparent and scientifically robust approaches to public health recommendations, free from the shadow of industry bias.

Conclusion

The story of the Food Pyramid serves as a vital lesson in the complex relationship between public health, scientific research, and industry interests. It underscores the need for critical evaluation and transparency in the development of nutritional guidelines. As we continue to navigate the intricate landscape of dietary advice, the legacy of the Food Pyramid reminds us to remain vigilant about the sources and motivations underpinning public health directives.

18

FDA revocation

In the intricate world of pharmaceuticals, the process of drug approval and subsequent revocation by the U.S. Food and Drug Administration (FDA) presents a profound ethical dilemma. This chapter explores the complex dynamics at play, including the significant influence of drug manufacturers and the vast number of Americans relying on medication, shedding light on the intricate balance between safeguarding public health and advancing medical science.

The FDA's Role Amidst Industry Influence

While the FDA is tasked with ensuring the safety and efficacy of medications, a critical ethical issue arises from the fact that drug manufacturers, driven by financial interests, provide much of the safety data used in the approval process. This relationship poses a potential conflict of interest, as these companies stand to gain significantly from the approval of their products, potentially affecting the objectivity of the data presented.

The Extent of Medication Use in the United States

The reliance on prescription medications in the United States is staggering. With over 66% of adults on prescription drugs, this translates to more than 131 million Americans dependent on the FDA's regulatory decisions for their health and well-being. This massive scale underscores the far-reaching impact of the FDA's decisions, amplifying the consequences of any lapses in the drug approval process.

Trust and Transparency

The dual issues of trust in the FDA and transparency from pharmaceutical companies form the crux of the ethical challenges in drug approval. Patients and healthcare providers place immense trust in the efficacy and safety of medications. However, this trust is challenged when safety concerns arise post-approval, often leading to drug revocations that affect millions.

The Reality of Revoked Drug Approvals

The withdrawal of drugs like Vioxx and Zelnorm highlights the ethical dilemma of weighing immediate medical requirements against long-term patient safety. These examples are not mere anomalies; they reflect a broader systemic problem wherein dependency on data provided by manufacturers can result in underrecognizing or minimizing risks. Research published in the Journal of the American Medical Association reveals that one-third of FDA-approved drugs eventually encounter safety issues. The consequences of these revocations are far-reaching, impacting not just physical health but also the psychological well-being of patients who must confront the unsettling truth that their medications might not be as safe as they were led to believe.

Reassessing the Approval Process

This reliance on industry-supplied data necessitates a reassessment of the drug approval process. The FDA, while operating under constraints, must navigate the delicate act of evaluating drugs efficiently while thoroughly scrutinizing the data, free from industry biases. This calls for enhanced independent testing and more stringent oversight to ensure that the health of the public is not compromised by commercial interests.

Ethical Vigilance and Patient Safety

The narrative of drug approval and revocation in the United States underscores the need for ethical vigilance in pharmaceutical regulation. As medical science progresses, so must the methodologies and ethical frameworks governing drug approvals. Ensuring patient safety requires a concerted effort towards transparency, unbiased research, and regulatory rigor.

Conclusion

The journey of a drug from development to market, and sometimes to revocation, is fraught with ethical complexities. The vast number of Americans on medication, coupled with the potential conflicts of interest in the drug approval process, paints a picture of a healthcare system in need of continuous ethical and regulatory refinement. The lessons drawn from past drug revocations should guide future policies and practices, ensuring that the pursuit of medical advancement never overshadows the paramount importance of patient safety and public trust.

19

CoVid-19 (2020)

The year 2020 marked a turning point in global health history with the outbreak of the COVID-19 pandemic and the rapid development of vaccines. This chapter explores the complex interplay between the urgency of addressing a global health crisis and the resultant rise in vaccine skepticism, set against a backdrop of historical mistrust in government actions.

The Pandemic's Unprecedented Challenge

Faced with the COVID-19 pandemic, a percieved extraordinary global health emergency, governments and scientific communities worldwide were propelled into action. The rapid development of vaccines, while a remarkable scientific achievement, occurred within compressed timelines, leading to questions about the thoroughness of testing and the long-term implications of these vaccines.

The Rise of Vaccine Skepticism

Historical instances of government overreach and lapses in the drug approval process contributed to public skepticism towards the COVID-19 vaccines. Concerns were amplified by the vaccines' expedited development and emergency use authorization, leading to fears about their long-term safety and efficacy. This skepticism was further fueled by censorship and de-platforming of dissenting voices, which, for many, raised red flags about transparency and the violation of informed consent principles as outlined in the Nuremberg Code.

Ethical Dilemmas and Rapid Response

The ethical challenges in the development of COVID-19 vaccines highlight the tension between the need for rapid medical solutions and the adherence to established scientific and ethical standards. The urgency to mitigate the pandemic's impact had to be weighed against the necessity of thorough, long-term safety evaluations, a process traditionally integral to vaccine development.

Contextualizing Skepticism in the Light of History

The skepticism surrounding the COVID-19 vaccines cannot be viewed in isolation but rather within the context of historical events where government actions caused unintended harm. This backdrop of mistrust necessitates a deeper understanding of public apprehensions and a commitment to addressing them through transparent and ethical practices.

Restoring Trust in Public Health

To restore public trust in health interventions, particularly vaccines, there is a need for transparent communication, robust safety monitoring, and respect for individual autonomy and consent. Building confidence in COVID-19 vaccines requires a concerted effort to address concerns, provide clear and consistent information, and engage with communities in an open and respectful manner.

Conclusion

The COVID-19 pandemic and the subsequent vaccine rollout have underscored the critical importance of trust in public health measures. The lessons learned during this period highlight the need for a balanced approach that prioritizes public safety while respecting individual rights and ethical standards. As we move forward, the legacy of COVID-19 vaccines serves as a reminder of the need for ongoing vigilance in maintaining ethical integrity in medical research and public health initiatives. By acknowledging and learning from past challenges, we can strengthen the foundation of trust and cooperation essential for tackling future health crises.

20

Part I Conclusion

"Betrayed Bodies: Government's Unauthorized Human Trials" concludes with a sobering reflection on the complex role of government in health and well-being. This exploration through history's darker corridors reveals a disturbing pattern of betrayal, unethical experimentation, and the erosion of trust in government institutions. These narratives compel us to critically evaluate the role of government in healthcare, especially in the context of historical transgressions.

Historical Betrayals and Unchecked Power

The chapters of this book have detailed instances where government actions prioritized expediency and secrecy over individual rights and well-being. From the Tuskegee Syphilis Study to the revocation of drug approvals, these cases illustrate the dangers of unchecked government power, highlighting the need for vigilance in preserving justice and individual autonomy.

Constitutional Considerations and Healthcare

The idea of federal involvement in healthcare raises significant constitutional concerns. The Constitution, with its emphasis on limited government powers and the protection of individual liberties, stands in contrast to the notion of a government-controlled healthcare system. Such control raises the specter of bureaucratic inefficiency, diminished personal choice, and weakened patient-doctor relationships.

The Shadows of Government Betrayal

The historical betrayals explored in this book serve as potent reminders of the risks inherent in granting extensive power to government institutions in healthcare decisions. These cautionary tales emphasize the need for transparency, informed consent, and a steadfast commitment to individual rights.

Merging Lessons from the Past with Present Vigilance

As we conclude this journey, we are faced with a pivotal question: Will we allow the mistakes of the past to be repeated, or will we strive to uphold the principles of a just and free society? The preservation of life, liberty, and dignity requires not just ethical research and conduct but also an enduring skepticism of government overreach.

Upholding Principles for the Future

In closing "Betrayed Bodies," we recognize the critical need for transparency, accountability, and the protection of individual autonomy. Our future hinges on our commitment to these principles, ensuring that the government respects its constitutional boundaries and empowers individuals in their health decisions. Only through a vigilant and informed citizenry can we prevent the repetition of past errors and foster a healthcare environment where individual choice and well-being are paramount.

II

Betrayed Liberties: Government's Erosion of Freedom

"Betrayed Liberties: Government's Erosion of Freedom," part two of "Trust Shattered," examines how governmental actions have eroded the freedoms meant to be protected. Highlighting infringements on speech and privacy, it uncovers the steps toward diminishing individual rights, balancing national security with liberty, and questioning the cost of safety at freedom's expense.

21

The Alien and Sedition Acts (1798)

The enactment of the Sedition Acts in 1798 represents a critical juncture in American history, where the ideals enshrined in the Bill of Rights, ratified merely seven years earlier, faced their first major test. This chapter examines the contradiction inherent in the passage of the Sedition Acts by a government that had so recently committed to protecting freedoms of speech and press.

Contextualizing the Sedition Acts

The Sedition Acts were part of a broader legislative effort, the Alien and Sedition Acts, passed during an era of political uncertainty and international tension. While the Alien Acts targeted non-citizens, the Sedition Acts directly impacted American citizens, criminalizing the publication of "false, scandalous, and malicious writing" against the government or its officials.

The Irony of Lawmakers' Involvement

Remarkably, several lawmakers who were instrumental in the crafting and ratification of the Bill of Rights played roles in the passage of the Sedition Acts. This contradiction underscores the complexities and shifting political landscapes of the era. It also reflects how quickly the principles of liberty can be compromised under the guise of national security and political expedience.

Victims of the Sedition Acts

The Sedition Acts led to the prosecution and imprisonment of numerous individuals, predominantly critics of the Federalist government:

- **Matthew Lyon**: A Democratic-Republican Congressman, Lyon was the first victim of the Sedition Acts. He was charged and imprisoned for writing a letter criticizing President John Adams's quest for power.
- **Thomas Cooper**: A lawyer and newspaper editor, Cooper was prosecuted for publishing a critical article about President Adams. His trial and subsequent conviction highlighted the Acts' direct assault on the freedom of the press.
- **James Callender**: A journalist known for his critical writings, Callender was another notable victim. His arrest and imprisonment under the Sedition Acts were emblematic of the government's efforts to silence dissent.

The Erosion of Liberty

The prosecutions under the Sedition Acts represented a significant erosion of the liberties that the Bill of Rights sought to protect. The acts challenged the core American values of free speech and a free press, leading to a period where political expression was met with fear and trepidation.

A Lesson in Liberty and Vigilance

The Sedition Acts serve as a powerful reminder of the fragility of civil liberties, especially during times of political unrest. They illustrate how quickly rights can be undermined by the very individuals entrusted with their protection. The Acts stand as a historical warning about the ease with which government can overstep its bounds, emphasizing the importance of constant vigilance in the defense of fundamental freedoms.

The legacy of the Sedition Acts is a testament to the need for a robust and enduring commitment to the principles enshrined in the Bill of Rights. As we reflect on this chapter of American history, we are reminded of the critical role of citizens in holding their government accountable and ensuring that the liberties guaranteed by the Constitution are never again so easily compromised.

22

Japanese Internment during World War II

The internment of Japanese-Americans during World War II remains a poignant example of the erosion of civil liberties in the face of national security fears. This chapter delves into the historical context, constitutional implications, and enduring lessons of this dark period in American history.

Pearl Harbor and its Aftermath

The Japanese attack on Pearl Harbor on December 7, 1941, plunged the United States into World War II and triggered a wave of fear and suspicion, particularly against the Japanese-American community. This fear, compounded by prejudice and political pressure, set the stage for one of the most significant civil liberties violations in American history.

Constitutional Framework and Executive Order 9066

In the constitutional landscape, the internment raises critical questions about the protection of civil liberties under the Fifth Amendment. President Roosevelt's Executive Order 9066, issued on February 19, 1942, authorized the forced relocation and internment of over 120,000 Japanese-Americans, the majority of whom were U.S. citizens. This decision, rooted more in racial prejudice than in any evidenced security threat, represented a stark deviation from the constitutional principles of liberty and equal protection.

Violation of Civil Liberties

The implementation of Executive Order 9066 led to profound violations of civil liberties. As Norman Mineta highlighted, Japanese-Americans were subjected to forced removal, loss of property, and years of life behind barbed wire, solely based on their ancestry. These actions disregarded the basic freedoms guaranteed by the Constitution, illustrating a disturbing case where fear and prejudice overrode the principles of justice and equality.

Supreme Court Upholds the Internment

The Supreme Court's decision in Korematsu v. United States (1944) further entrenched this injustice. The court's ruling, which declared the internment constitutional, was a critical moment where judicial oversight failed to protect individual rights against governmental overreach. Justice Hugo Black's rationale of "military necessity" highlighted a troubling prioritization of perceived security over personal liberties.

The Aftermath and Apology

The end of World War II in 1945 marked the conclusion of the internment, but its impact lingered for decades. The recognition of the injustice came significantly later, with the U.S. government formally acknowledging its mistake through the Civil Liberties Act of 1988. President Ronald Reagan's apology and the reparations to surviving internees were crucial steps in addressing the wrongs, yet they could not fully undo the damage inflicted upon the Japanese-American community.

Lessons for the Future

The internment of Japanese-Americans is a stark reminder of the perils of allowing fear and prejudice to dictate government policy. It underscores the importance of upholding civil liberties, even in times of crisis, and the need for constant vigilance against the infringement of these rights. This episode in history serves as a cautionary tale, reminding us that the principles of justice and equality must guide our actions, even in the face of national security concerns.

As Mahatma Gandhi's words remind us, the greatness of a nation lies in how it treats its most vulnerable members. Reflecting on this period urges us to ensure that the mistakes of the past are not repeated and that the rights and freedoms of all individuals are respected, irrespective of their ethnicity or background. The legacy of Executive Order 9066 teaches us the importance of safeguarding civil liberties for all, to maintain the integrity of our constitutional values and the principles upon which the United States was founded.

23

McCarthyism and the Red Scare (1950s)

McCarthyism, marked by its anti-communist crusade and political repression, is a pivotal chapter in the history of American civil liberties. This era, ignited by the Red Scare of the 1950s, exemplifies the consequences of allowing fear, prejudice, and unchecked political power to erode the foundational rights of American citizens.

Historical Context and Political Climate

In the post-World War II era, America found itself grappling with the rise of the Cold War and the perceived threat of communism. This period of heightened anxiety laid the groundwork for Senator Joseph McCarthy's rise to prominence. McCarthy's campaign against alleged communist infiltration tapped into deep-seated fears, creating a climate ripe for political repression.

Constitutional Framework

The tactics employed during McCarthyism stand in stark contrast to the constitutional protections promised in the Bill of Rights. The widespread persecution and violation of civil liberties under McCarthy's watch challenged the very essence of the First Amendment rights to free speech and association. The era highlighted a fundamental constitutional crisis: the balancing act between safeguarding national security and preserving individual freedoms.

Tactics Employed and Impact on Civil Liberties

McCarthyism was characterized by aggressive investigations and blacklisting, targeting not only government employees but also individuals in the entertainment industry and beyond. The House Un-American Activities Committee (HUAC) played a central role in this persecution, often employing guilt by association, character assassination, and unsubstantiated accusations as tools for political repression.

The impact on civil liberties was profound and far-reaching. Individuals accused of communist sympathies faced career destruction, social ostracization, and in some cases, imprisonment. The climate of fear and suspicion fostered during this time stifled free expression and thought, directly contradicting the principles of a free society.

Long-Term Effects and Modern Parallels

The legacy of McCarthyism extends beyond the 1950s, leaving an indelible mark on American society and politics. The era serves as a stark reminder of how fear can be exploited for political gain, often at the expense of fundamental liberties. Today, parallels can be drawn to instances where activism and dissent are met with suspicion and suppression, echoing the tactics of McCarthyism.

Confronting McCarthy and the Army-McCarthy Hearings

The Army-McCarthy hearings, televised and widely watched, played a pivotal role in exposing the baseless nature of Mc-Carthy's claims and the recklessness of his methods. These hearings marked a turning point in public perception, showcasing the importance of transparency and accountability in preserving constitutional values. The downfall of McCarthy, culminating in his condemnation by the Senate, was a testament to the resilience of American democracy and the ultimate triumph of justice over fear-mongering and demagoguery.

Conclusion

McCarthyism and the Red Scare era serve as potent reminders of the delicate balance between protecting national security and upholding civil liberties. They underscore the importance of remaining vigilant against the erosion of constitutional rights, especially in times of fear and uncertainty. As we reflect on this chapter of American history, we recognize the need to safeguard our liberties, resist the temptation to stifle dissent, and uphold the principles of justice and fairness. By learning from the past, we can ensure a future where the rights and freedoms of all citizens are respected and protected.

24

COINTELPRO (1956-1971)

COINTELPRO, the FBI's Counterintelligence Program, is a stark example of government overreach infringing upon civil liberties under the pretext of national security. From 1956 to 1971, this series of covert and illegal projects targeted a wide array of political organizations and activists, revealing the extent to which the government was willing to go to suppress dissent.

Historical Context and Political Climate

The origins of COINTELPRO can be traced back to the Cold War era, a time marked by intense fear of communism and perceived threats to American values. The program's emergence was fueled by the political climate of the time, with the Soviet Union's atomic capabilities and the spread of communism worldwide heightening the sense of urgency to protect national security.

Constitutional Implications

COINTELPRO's actions were in direct violation of constitutional protections, including the First Amendment rights of free speech and assembly and the Fourth Amendment rights against unreasonable searches and seizures. The program represents a grave encroachment on civil liberties and a significant deviation from the constitutional principles upon which the United States was founded.

Tactics Employed by the FBI

The FBI's methods in COINTELPRO included psychological warfare, infiltration of groups, harassment, and illegal violence. These tactics were aimed at discrediting and disrupting political organizations. Notable targets included civil rights activists, feminist groups, and anti-war protestors, with the FBI often resorting to egregious measures to achieve its objectives.

Impact on Political Activism and Freedom of Speech

The program had a chilling effect on political activism and freedom of speech. The fear and paranoia instigated by COINTELPRO led to self-censorship and a significant decrease in political engagement among groups that were targeted. Activists and organizations faced not only the threat of surveillance but also the potential of being publicly discredited or worse, becoming victims of illegal violence. This atmosphere stifled the free exchange of ideas and undermined the democratic process.

The Exposure of COINTELPRO

The revelation of COINTELPRO in 1971, following the burglary of an FBI office by the Citizens' Commission to Investigate the FBI, was a pivotal moment in American history. The public was shocked to learn about the extent of the FBI's covert activities. This exposure led to a national outcry for accountability and reform, highlighting the need for oversight in government agencies.

Violations of Civil Liberties and Constitutional Rights

COINTELPRO's operations were a clear breach of constitutional rights, particularly those related to privacy, free speech, and due process. The program's tactics not only violated the legal rights of individuals but also the moral and ethical standards expected in a free society. These actions demonstrated a disturbing willingness by the government to prioritize perceived national security interests over the fundamental rights of its citizens.

The Legacy and Continued Relevance

The legacy of COINTELPRO continues to resonate today. It serves as a reminder of the dangers posed by unchecked government surveillance and the importance of safeguarding civil liberties, especially in times of national crisis. The program's impact extends into contemporary discussions about government surveillance, privacy rights, and the balance between security and freedom.

Ongoing Efforts for Reform and Prevention

The exposure of COINTELPRO has led to ongoing efforts to reform government surveillance practices and ensure the protection of civil liberties. These efforts include advocating for stronger oversight of intelligence agencies, enhancing legal protections for privacy and free speech, and promoting transparency in government operations.

Conclusion

COINTELPRO's history is a cautionary tale about the potential for government abuse of power and the necessity of constant vigilance in protecting freedoms. As we move forward, it is crucial to remember the lessons learned from this dark chapter in American history, ensuring that such violations of civil liberties and constitutional rights are never repeated.

25

NSA Surveillance (ongoing)

The National Security Agency's (NSA) surveillance program vividly illustrates the tension between national security and individual privacy, highlighting a significant betrayal of public trust. Initiated under the guise of protecting national interests, the program's extensive and invasive surveillance capabilities—cataloged and exposed by whistleblower Edward Snowden—have sparked a national and global debate on privacy, freedom, and the role of government in the digital age.

Constitutional Concerns and the Erosion of Privacy

At the heart of the controversy is the stark contradiction between the NSA's expansive data collection methods and the Fourth Amendment's protection against unreasonable searches and seizures. The indiscriminate gathering of phone records, emails, and internet activities by the NSA, often without targeted warrants or clear oversight, raises alarm about the overreach of state power and its implications for personal freedoms. Snowden's disclosures not only unveiled the depth of surveillance but also its broader implications for free speech, expression, and democratic engagement, igniting a reevaluation of privacy rights in the 21st century.

The Culture of Surveillance and Its Impacts

The revelations about the NSA's activities have significantly damaged public trust in governmental institutions, fostering a culture of skepticism and fear. This environment, where surveillance abuses can proliferate unchecked, undermines the foundational principles of privacy and freedom, leading to self-censorship among citizens wary of overreaching government scrutiny. The knowledge of being under constant watch has stifled innovation, restricted civil liberties, and altered the fabric of societal interactions.

Urgent Need for Surveillance Reform

The history of government surveillance in the United States, marked by programs like PRISM and the bulk collection of phone metadata, reveals a disturbing trajectory toward increased surveillance and control. These examples of overreach underscore the critical need for comprehensive reforms to ensure that surveillance is conducted lawfully, with genuine respect for privacy and individual rights. Measures such as stricter warrant requirements, improved judicial oversight, and enhanced transparency are pivotal in reestablishing a foundation of trust and accountability between the government and the public.

Balancing National Security with Individual Rights

The challenge of reconciling the demands of national security with the imperative to protect individual freedoms is ongoing. It necessitates a vigilant, adaptive legal framework that can respond to technological advancements and evolving threats without compromising the civil liberties that underpin a free and open society.

A Path Forward: Preserving Privacy in the Digital Age

To effectively address the challenges presented by mass surveillance, a multifaceted approach involving legal, technological, and societal efforts is essential. Innovations in technology that safeguard privacy, coupled with an active public discourse on the limits of surveillance, are crucial for crafting a future that honors both security and liberty.

In conclusion, the NSA's surveillance program underscores the paramount importance of vigilantly defending civil liberties against encroachments in the name of security. Through informed engagement, legal reforms, and ethical technological practices, society can navigate the complexities of modern security challenges while steadfastly protecting the individual freedoms that constitute the essence of democratic governance. As we move forward, let us commit to a vision of society that holds the rights enshrined in our Constitution not merely as ideals but as active principles to be vigorously defended.

26

Patriot Act (2001)

The USA PATRIOT Act, swiftly enacted in the immediate aftermath of the September 11, 2001, terrorist attacks, epitomizes a pivotal moment when the United States government, driven by a mix of fear and determination to prevent future attacks, chose to significantly expand its surveillance capabilities at the expense of civil liberties. This legislation, born out of a national crisis, was pitched as an essential tool in the war on terror. Yet, it has since become a controversial cornerstone in the debate over the balance between national security and individual privacy rights, highlighting a profound shift in the landscape of American civil liberties.

The Aftermath of 9/11 and Legislative Response

The devastating attacks of 9/11 created an atmosphere of fear and urgency that led to the rapid passage of the PATRIOT Act. The Act was intended to arm law enforcement and intelligence agencies with new tools to combat terrorism. However, the speed with which it was pushed through Congress meant that there was little opportunity for debate or consideration of its broader implications for privacy and freedom. This legislative haste set a precedent for the erosion of constitutional protections in the name of security.

Expanding Surveillance and Eroding Privacy

Central to the controversy surrounding the PATRIOT Act is its authorization of sweeping surveillance practices that infringe upon the Fourth Amendment's protections against unreasonable searches and seizures. The Act facilitated warrantless wiretapping, bulk data collection, and the use of National Security Letters (NSLs) to obtain personal records without a court order—measures that significantly widened the scope of government surveillance and encroached on the privacy of American citizens.

The Use and Abuse of National Security Letters

The employment of NSLs under the PATRIOT Act is particularly emblematic of the Act's overreach. These letters grant federal agencies the power to demand personal information from banks, telephone companies, and other entities without prior judicial approval, effectively sidestepping traditional checks and balances. The secretive nature of NSLs and the prohibition against disclosure to the individuals under investigation have raised serious due process concerns and highlighted the potential for abuse within the surveillance apparatus.

A Divided Nation: Security Versus Civil Liberties

The enactment and subsequent reauthorizations of the PA-TRIOT Act, despite clear constitutional violations, have revealed deep divisions within American society regarding the trade-offs between national security and individual freedoms. While some view the Act's provisions as necessary sacrifices in the fight against terrorism, others argue that they represent a dangerous precedent for the curtailment of civil liberties—a slippery slope toward a surveillance state.

Reflections on the Legacy and Path Forward

The legacy of the USA PATRIOT Act is a complex tapestry of intent, impact, and controversy. It serves as a stark reminder of the challenges democracies face in times of crisis: how to protect the nation while also safeguarding the freedoms upon which it was founded. As we move forward, the lessons learned from the implementation and criticisms of the PATRIOT Act must inform future legislative and policy decisions, ensuring that measures to enhance security do not come at the unacceptable cost of eroding fundamental civil liberties.

In conclusion, the USA PATRIOT Act represents a critical juncture in American history, where the response to a national tragedy led to significant, and in many ways troubling, changes in the relationship between the government and its citizens. Its story is a cautionary tale of how the noble pursuit of security can sometimes lead to the unintended consequence of undermining the very freedoms it seeks to protect. As a nation, our enduring challenge is to navigate the delicate balance between security and freedom, ensuring that our responses to threats do not compromise the constitutional rights and liberties that define us.

27

Censorship and Internet Regulation (ongoing)

In the digital age, the intersection of free speech and government regulation has become a battleground for the principles enshrined in the First Amendment. While the internet has democratized information dissemination, facilitating an explosion of expression and ideas, it has also opened the door for governmental attempts to control or influence the narrative under the guise of security, decency, or combating misinformation. This chapter delves into the intricate dance between preserving the sanctity of free speech and navigating government actions that threaten to undermine it, particularly through the indirect censorship leveraged by private entities.

The Digital Revolution and the First Amendment

The inception of the internet, a byproduct of government innovation, has blossomed into a vital arena for free expression, hosting a cacophony of voices from every corner of the globe.

This remarkable expansion of communicative freedom, however, has paradoxically enticed government surveillance and oversight, posing significant challenges to First Amendment guarantees. The essence of free speech, a cornerstone of American freedom, is at risk of being diluted by governmental overreach masquerading as regulatory oversight.

Governmental Overreach in the Digital Sphere

As digital platforms have become central to public discourse, the government's inclination to regulate content has intensified. Attempts to curtail speech, under the premise of national security or public morality, often conflict directly with First Amendment protections. Governmental directives to suppress or manipulate online content—save for that which is explicitly illegal—constitute a breach of constitutional rights. This form of censorship, whether direct or indirect, not only stifles innovation and expression but also sets a dangerous precedent for the erosion of fundamental liberties.

The Complicity of Private Entities

The modern conundrum of content moderation on digital platforms introduces a complex layer to the debate over free speech. While private companies like social media giants possess the right to enforce their own content policies, the waters become muddied when these policies intersect with government interests or pressures. This collaboration, or at times coercion, between the state and private sector to censor or shape discourse underlines a troubling trend toward indirect government censorship. Such maneuvers not only challenge the autonomy of these platforms but also endanger the public's right to access diverse viewpoints and information.

Defining the Limits: Illegal Speech

The regulation of speech by the government is constitutionally limited to certain illegal categories, such as incitement to violence, threats, and obscenity. These narrowly defined exceptions are critical in maintaining a balance between ensuring public safety and upholding free expression. However, the expansion of surveillance practices, often justified under the broad umbrella of national security, has encroached upon privacy rights, indirectly chilling speech and eroding the foundational principle of anonymity in discourse.

The Global Challenge of Regulating Online Speech

The ubiquity of the internet transcends national boundaries, complicating the governance of online speech. While individual countries grapple with their domestic policies, there's an emerging need for a global dialogue to establish norms that respect free expression while curbing illegal content. The quest for an international consensus on these matters underscores the tension between sovereignty and universal human rights.

Net Neutrality and the Preservation of Open Access

The principle of net neutrality is vital in ensuring that the internet remains a level playing field, where information flows freely without preferential treatment or suppression by Internet Service Providers or government mandates. Protecting this openness is paramount in safeguarding the diversity of thought and expression that characterizes the internet.

Navigating the Future

As we venture further into the digital era, the imperative to reevaluate and adapt our approach to free speech and government intervention becomes increasingly apparent. Upholding the prohibition against government-directed censorship, outside the realm of illegal speech, is essential in maintaining the integrity of our democratic values. The vigilance of citizens, policymakers, and the courts is necessary to ensure that the evolving landscape of digital communication fosters a society where freedom of expression thrives alongside responsible governance.

In conclusion, the challenges presented by the digital age call for a nuanced understanding of the delicate balance between free speech and governmental responsibility. The NSA surveillance program's revelations, alongside the broader issues of online censorship and content regulation, serve as a stark reminder of the ongoing battle to protect individual liberties in the face of security concerns. It is our collective responsibility to champion the principles of the First Amendment, ensuring that the digital public square remains a bastion of free and open discourse.

28

Permission Society

The transition towards a "Permission Society" marks a pivotal shift where governmental approval becomes a central aspect of daily existence. This chapter delves into the deep impacts of this change, emphasizing the growing tension between an enlarging regulatory apparatus and the core values of personal freedom.

Understanding Licensing Complexities

- **Professional Licensing:** While meant to guarantee public safety and quality, the requirements for professional licenses have ironically turned into significant barriers. These barriers restrict career paths in various sectors, from healthcare to beauty, through a complicated set of prerequisites that deter aspiring professionals, limit consumer choices, and hinder the accessibility of services.
- **Business Licensing:** Aimed at ensuring public safety and adherence to regulations, business licensing can result in undue government intervention. This excessive oversight

disproportionately affects small businesses and new ventures, stifling innovation due to the burdens of compliance costs and regulatory hurdles.

- **Marriage Licensing:** The requirement for official marriage licenses encroaches upon personal relationships, illustrating how far regulatory influence extends into private lives and questioning the need for such control in intimate choices.
- **Recreational Licensing:** Licensing for activities like hunting and fishing, while meant for environmental preservation, raises concerns about the encroachment on property rights and the freedoms of landowners, even with conservation objectives in mind.
- **Speech Permits:** The necessity for permits to hold public gatherings challenges the principles of free speech and assembly, ostensibly for public safety reasons but with the potential to suppress democratic engagement and protest.

The Pervasive Role of Regulations

The gradual expansion of government rules into various life areas raises concerns about the erosion of individual liberties. Though intended to protect health, safety, and consumer interests, the overall impact of these regulations severely restricts personal freedom, ranging from the licensing of pets and vehicles to the control over marriage, careers, and hobbies, indicating a move towards a society based on obtaining permission.

Addressing the Challenges

The Permission Society necessitates a thoughtful examination of the balance between personal freedoms and the needs of the community. It is crucial to evaluate the consequences of widespread regulations, aiming for a society that places public well-being at the forefront without sacrificing the principles of freedom and autonomy.

Urging Reassessment and Reform

In navigating the complexities of contemporary governance, it is vital to remain vigilant and proactive in advocating for a regulatory framework that minimizes unnecessary government intrusion while upholding the principles of freedom and self-governance. The Permission Society serves as both a cautionary tale and a catalyst for change, encouraging a reevaluation of our path to ensure that individual rights are protected against the encroaching tide of regulatory oversight.

29

Victimless Crimes

America, the land of liberty, stands at a crossroads. While we champion individual freedom, our justice system grapples with a stark contradiction: the mass incarceration of individuals for actions that don't directly harm others. This paradox, dubbed "victimless crimes," demands critical examination. This chapter delves deeper, unveiling its historical roots, analyzing its devastating consequences, and advocating for a path towards a more just and restorative system.

Defining the Spectrum

"Victimless crimes" is a loaded term, obscuring the diverse actions it encompasses. From personal substance use to consensual adult sex work, unauthorized gambling, and certain traffic infractions, each carries its own story. Let's move beyond the label and explore the nuances within this spectrum. While acknowledging potential indirect societal impacts, remember the absence of direct victims – a crucial distinction fueling the ongoing debate about legal boundaries and individual liberties.

Morality vs. Freedom

The roots of criminalizing victimless crimes lie in a tangled history. Societal norms, religious ideals, and political agendas intertwined to shape legal statutes. Public morality and social order often trumped individual freedoms, raising questions about the true "compass" guiding these laws. As the debate continues, we must critically examine the ethical justifications for state intervention in personal choices.

The War on Drugs

The War on Drugs offers a chilling case study. It demonstrates the devastating consequences of criminalizing victimless crimes. Mass incarceration, disproportionately impacting minorities, for minor drug offenses exposes systemic flaws. This failed policy demands a critical reassessment. We must shift towards rehabilitation, restorative justice, and evidence-based approaches that prioritize societal well-being over punitive measures.

Beyond Incarceration

The impact of victimless crimes extends far beyond individual incarceration. Broken families, marginalized communities, and the colossal financial burden of maintaining an expansive prison system represent the hidden costs. Social mobility, employment opportunities, and overall community well-being suffer. We must acknowledge this ripple effect and seek solutions that not only address individual choices but also strengthen the fabric of society.

The Legal and Ethical Labyrinth

Navigating the legal and ethical complexities of victimless crimes requires navigating a labyrinth. The right to individual liberty clashes with the government's responsibility for public safety, raising intricate questions about the proper scope of law and its effectiveness in addressing societal issues. Decriminalization and alternative approaches emerge as viable solutions, necessitating careful consideration of their potential and limitations.

From Reform to Restoration

Instead of viewing punishment solely through the lens of incarceration, let's explore the transformative potential of community service. Unlike prison, community service allows individuals to contribute meaningfully to the society they've allegedly "wronged." By repairing parks, assisting the elderly, or mentoring youth, they become participants in their own rehabilitation and societal repair. This restorative approach fosters accountability, responsibility, and a sense of belonging, breaking the cycle of punishment and offering a truly just alternative.

Reclaiming the Promise of Justice:

Victimless crimes challenge the core principles of justice and freedom. It's time for a nuanced reassessment of laws that disproportionately penalize non-violent behaviors. We must advocate for a system that prioritizes:

- **Rehabilitation over punishment:** Empowering individuals to become productive members of society, not burdening them with a lifelong stigma.
- **Equality over disparity:** Ensuring equal justice for all, regardless of race, ethnicity, or socioeconomic background.
- **Individual rights over intrusion:** Upholding individual liberties while recognizing the state's legitimate role in promoting public safety and well-being.

By embracing reform, including the transformative power of community service, we can foster a society that truly honors the dignity, liberty, and well-being of all its members. This is the path towards a more just and truly free society, one that keeps its promise for all.

30

Right to Protest

The right to protest is the heartbeat of a free society, yet increasingly, a bureaucratic hurdle stands in its way: the protest permit. While ostensibly aimed at maintaining order and safety, permit requirements often morph into instruments of restriction, potentially silencing dissent and jeopardizing a fundamental democratic right. This chapter delves into this complex landscape, exploring the inherent problems with mandated permits for protests and their chilling effect on free expression.

From Open Streets to Permitting Maze:

Imagine the vibrant tapestry of a protest – spontaneous, passionate, a kaleidoscope of voices demanding change. Now, overlay it with the bureaucratic grid of a permit application: timelines, fees, detailed route maps, sound limitations. The once dynamic protest shrinks into a pre-approved, sanitized version, its spontaneity and urgency stifled. This is the reality for protestors navigating the labyrinthine permit systems increasingly imposed by local authorities.

The Two Sides of the Permitting Coin

Proponents claim permits ensure public safety and minimize disruption. They envision orderly gatherings, manageable traffic flow, and pre-emptive measures to address potential security threats. Opponents see a different picture: unnecessary hurdles, restrictive conditions, and the potential for unfettered discretion in granting or denying permits, particularly when addressing unpopular viewpoints.

Chilling the Right to Dissent

The very existence of permit requirements can have a chilling effect on potential protestors. The fear of complex procedures, potential denials, and hefty fees can dissuade individuals and groups from exercising their right to assemble and express dissent. This chilling effect disproportionately impacts marginalized communities and grassroots movements who may lack the resources to navigate the permitting process.

The Weaponization of Bureaucracy

Concerns mount when permit applications become tools for selective silencing. Authorities, particularly those opposed to the protest's message, may impose unreasonable restrictions, delay approvals, or deny permits altogether. This weaponization of the permitting process undermines the very foundation of free speech and assembly, creating a system where protests become privileges granted, not rights enshrined.

Seeking a Middle Ground

Finding a workable solution requires balancing public safety concerns with the fundamental right to protest. Exploring alternatives like notification systems instead of permits, clear standards for permit approvals, and transparency in decision-making processes can offer a path forward. Open dialogue between authorities, community groups, and legal experts is crucial to crafting regulations that uphold public safety without sacrificing the essence of protest.

The Unfinished Symphony

The battle over protest permits remains an ongoing struggle. As societies grapple with evolving social and political landscapes, ensuring the right to protest thrives in the face of bureaucratic hurdles is paramount. This is not just about safeguarding a legal right; it's about ensuring the symphony of dissent continues to play its vital role in a healthy democracy. We must strive for a harmonious balance, where legitimate concerns for public safety coexist with the unfettered expression of voices demanding change.

31

COVID-19 Pandemic

The COVID-19 pandemic, emerging in late 2019, presented unprecedented challenges to personal liberties, foregrounding critical questions about government roles during health crises. This chapter examines the fine line between individual freedoms and public health imperatives during the pandemic.

The Onset of the Pandemic

The novel coronavirus outbreak, originating in Wuhan, China, rapidly evolved into a global crisis. Governments worldwide, grappling with this unforeseen emergency, implemented measures to mitigate its spread, significantly impacting personal liberties and societal norms.

Government Responses and Personal Liberties

The array of measures taken—ranging from mask mandates to lockdowns—highlighted the inherent tension between collective health goals and individual rights. These actions, aimed at safeguarding public health, often came at the cost of personal freedom and choice, igniting widespread debate.

Mask Mandates: A Freedom of Choice Dilemma

Mandatory mask-wearing policies became a focal point of contention. Proponents viewed them as simple, effective public health tools, while opponents saw them as overreaches of government power, often enforced through fines and arrests, deepening the rift over personal autonomy.

Economic Fallout and Lockdown Decisions

The enforcement of government-mandated business closures wreaked havoc on the economy, disproportionately impacting small businesses. While these local enterprises were forced to close their doors, major corporations continued to operate, spotlighting a stark disparity in treatment. This approach not only raises serious concerns about the fairness of government intervention in the economy but also underscores a glaring violation of property rights. By allowing large chains to remain open while small businesses were compelled to shut down, the government infringed on the financial freedom and rights of small business owners, highlighting an unjust application of regulatory measures.

Vaccine Mandates and Privacy Rights

The introduction of vaccines and subsequent enforcement of vaccination mandates by governments and employers magnified concerns over medical privacy violations, particularly under HIPAA, and individual autonomy. These mandates, requiring disclosure of vaccination status, led to numerous individuals losing their jobs for non-compliance, exacerbating worries about the erosion of the right to private health decisions.

Science, Trust, and Government Skepticism

The degree of public trust in government and scientific institutions significantly influenced the responses to the pandemic. Nevertheless, a deep-rooted skepticism towards government-directed health policies, extensively examined in Part 1 of this book, has fostered widespread hesitancy and resistance. This skepticism, stemming from past instances where government actions have fallen short or betrayed public trust, has made it challenging to achieve widespread compliance with public health directives, thereby hampering efforts to manage the pandemic efficiently.

Emergency Powers and Civil Liberties

The widespread use of emergency powers by governments in response to the pandemic has spotlighted a critical point: there is no "emergency exception" to the rights guaranteed by the Constitution. While claimed to be crucial for crisis management, these powers have sparked intense debate over their broad scope, arbitrary application, and indefinite extension, underscoring the urgent necessity for stringent oversight and accountability. This situation serves as a reminder that even in times of crisis, the principles of liberty and constitutionally protected rights remain non-negotiable.

Striking a Balance

The pandemic highlighted the complexities of balancing public health imperatives with the preservation of individual freedoms. The decisions and policies enacted during this period underlined the ongoing challenge of navigating the fine line between necessary government intervention and the protection of personal liberties.

Lessons for Future Public Health Crises

The COVID-19 pandemic serves as a critical learning point for future public health emergencies. It underscores the importance of transparent, science-based decision-making, respectful of individual rights while addressing collective health needs. The experience also emphasizes the need for clear communication and trust-building strategies to ensure public cooperation and compliance.

Reflecting on Governance and Liberty

"The health of a democratic society may be measured by the quality of functions performed by private citizens." - Alexis de Tocqueville

The pandemic has reignited vital discussions about the government's role in managing public health crises and the implications for individual rights. As we move forward, it is essential to reflect on these lessons, striving to establish a governance framework that respects personal freedoms while effectively responding to collective health needs. Ensuring this balance will be pivotal in preserving the foundational values of liberty and freedom in the face of future challenges.

32

January 6th, 2021

January 6th, 2021, remains a contentious and divisive chapter in American history. While some characterize it as an insurrection, others view it as a protest gone awry. Regardless of perspective, the aftermath of that day has had far-reaching implications, raising concerns about the erosion of fundamental constitutional principles. This chapter delves into the impact of January 6th on individual liberties, examining the erosion of Fourth, Sixth, Eighth, and Fourteenth Amendment rights.

Historical Context

On January 6th, 2021, an estimated 120,000 people were at Capitol Hill to protest irregularities they believed were signs of a stolen election. Law enforcement was woefully unprepared for the sheer number of attendees, even though national news outlets were reporting the expectation for at least a week before the planned protest.

On one side of the Capitol building, violence broke out.

Some protesters turned into rioters and forced their way inside the building. These violent videos were played repeatedly by mainstream media outlets.

On the other side of the Capitol building, police removed barriers and allowed protesters to enter the Capitol. Security videos show police moving barricades, protesters peacefully walking between velvet ropes, and posing for pictures with police. Mainstream media did not widely share these videos.

Jacob Chansley, known as the QAnon Shaman, was sentenced to 41 months in federal prison even though there is a video of him receiving a police escort through the halls of Congress and calling for his fellow protesters to respect the space and remain peaceful. The jury was not allowed to see those videos.

In November 2023, the House of Representatives released more security videos. Many of these videos show protesters peacefully walking past Capitol Police Officers who were not trying to stop the protesters. These videos were not available as evidence for any of the defendants tried thus far.

Newly released footage from January 6, 2021, shows Matthew Perna calmly strolling through the building alongside other protesters and even many police officers. Perna killed himself after prosecutors in his case added a terrorism enhancement in advance of his sentencing. Perna is one of over a dozen protesters who have taken their own lives.

Affects on Liberty

Fourth Amendment

"The right of the people to be secure in their persons, houses, papers, and effects, against unreasonable searches and seizures, shall not be violated, and no Warrants shall issue, but upon probable cause, supported by Oath or affirmation, and particularly describing the place to be searched, and the persons or things to be seized." - Fourth Amendment to the US Constitution

In the aftermath, extensive intrusive surveillance methods by the Federal Bureau of Investigation employed cell phone location data, credit card transactions, and airline flight information without adherence to constitutional standards. This mass data collection, enabled by National Security Letters under the Patriot Act, raises concerns about privacy and individual liberties, a departure from the Fourth Amendment's protections against unreasonable searches and seizures. Thousands of people were interviewed, and hundreds were arrested within weeks. Facial recognition software was applied to the thousands of hours of security video, and hundreds more were arrested.

Sixth Amendment

"In all criminal prosecutions, the accused shall enjoy the right to a speedy and public trial, by an impartial jury of the State and district wherein the crime shall have been committed, which district shall have been previously ascertained by law, and to be informed of the nature and cause of the accusation; to be confronted with

the witnesses against him; to have compulsory process for obtaining witnesses in his favor, and to have the Assistance of Counsel for his defence."- Sixth amendment to the US Constitution

The right to a speedy trial, a cornerstone safeguard against government overreach, has been compromised for several individuals associated with the events of January 6th, 2021. As of November 2023, some defendants languish in federal prison for over 1,000 days without standing trial, a clear violation of their Sixth Amendment rights.

According to the Bureau of Prisons, at least one defendant, Samuel Lazar, was sentenced in Washington's federal court to 30 months in prison, but there's no public record of such a hearing. That is definitely not a public trial.

Many defendants and their attorneys have reported being denied the right to cross-examine witnesses. Some witnesses told stories on the stand that contradicted their previous statements to law enforcement. Without cross-examination, the juries are unaware of these contradictory statements.

Much of the security videos of that day have not been made available to defense teams, and much of what has been made available has been denied admission as evidence, further undermining the principles of fair and public trials. The same government prosecuting the accused owns thousands of hours of video footage from that day. Denying the defense access to this footage is a clear violation of the rules of discovery and handling of exculpatory evidence.

Eighth Amendment

"Excessive bail shall not be required, nor excessive fines imposed, nor cruel and unusual punishments inflicted." - Eighth Amendment to the US Constitution

The excessive and prolonged detention of accused individuals, often held in solitary confinement without bail for extended periods, raises questions about the application of the Eighth Amendment. Many detainees, lacking criminal records and including military veterans, face conditions inconsistent with the prohibition of cruel and unusual punishment. Many were held for years without being allowed to see their families, even via Zoom, until their trial.

Fourteenth Amendment

"...nor shall any State deprive any person of life, liberty, or property, without due process of law; nor deny to any person within its jurisdiction the equal protection of the laws." - Fourteenth Amendment to the US Constitution

The prisoners of January 6th, 2021, have been denied their fundamental rights to life, liberty, and property without due process of law. The unequal application of due process is evident in the stark contrast between the treatment of these defendants in Washington DC jurisdiction and the leniency towards violent criminals within the city, where cash bail is lowered or eliminated.

The aftermath of January 6th, 2021, has cast a long shadow over the American legal system. The erosion of constitutional principles, particularly the Fourth, Sixth, Eighth, and Fourteenth Amendments, raises concerns about all Americans' fundamental rights and protections. Whether these prisoners are patriots, insurrectionists, or both; it is imperative to uphold these principles and ensure that the equal application of justice aligns with the foundational values of the United States.

33

Part II Conclusion

As we conclude our examination of government actions that have eroded individual liberties, a disquieting pattern emerges. This narrative, spanning from historical events to contemporary issues, highlights the disturbing ease and frequency with which government institutions can overstep their bounds, infringing upon the very freedoms they are meant to protect.

Summarizing Government Attacks on Liberty

Throughout this exploration, we have witnessed various instances where government actions have compromised personal freedoms. From the Alien & Sedition Acts to the NSA surveillance program, and from COINTELPRO to the complexities of the COVID-19 pandemic response, each chapter has revealed different facets of governmental overreach. These events demonstrate a recurring theme: the tension between state power and individual rights, and the vulnerability of the latter in times of perceived crisis or political expedience.

The Disturbing Ease and Frequency of Betrayals

A troubling aspect of these historical and contemporary examples is the ease with which liberties can be compromised under the guise of national security, public order, or even public health. Often, these infringements occur incrementally, making them less noticeable and more easily accepted by the public. This gradual erosion of rights, coupled with the frequency of such occurrences, underscores the need for constant vigilance in the defense of personal freedoms.

The Necessity of Knowing and Protecting Your Rights

The key to guarding against these betrayals lies in a deep understanding and appreciation of our rights. Knowledge of one's rights under the Constitution is not just academic; it is a practical necessity for safeguarding personal liberties. It is incumbent upon each citizen to be informed, to question, and to challenge governmental actions that encroach upon these rights.

The Role of Civic Engagement and Advocacy

Active civic engagement and advocacy play crucial roles in protecting liberties. Participation in democratic processes, critical scrutiny of government policies, and support for organizations that fight for civil rights are all vital in ensuring that government power is checked and balanced. It is through collective action and informed discourse that liberties can be effectively safeguarded.

A Call to Uphold Constitutional Ideals

In conclusion, the history of government overreach serves as a powerful reminder of the fragility of our liberties. As we move forward, it becomes increasingly clear that the protection of individual rights is not just the responsibility of the courts or lawmakers, but of every citizen. Vigilance, education, and active participation in the democratic process are essential in preventing the recurrence of past mistakes.

Our liberties, enshrined in the Constitution, provide the foundation for a free and just society. It is through understanding these rights and actively defending them that we ensure the preservation of liberty for ourselves and future generations. Let this reflection on government overreach serve as a catalyst for a renewed commitment to these fundamental principles.

In the words of James Madison, "Knowledge will forever govern ignorance; and a people who mean to be their own governors must arm themselves with the power which knowledge gives." It is through this knowledge and a steadfast commitment to our constitutionally guaranteed rights that we can safeguard our liberties against any form of governmental betrayal.

III

Betrayed Estates: Property's Conquest by Authority

In the annals of human history, the right to property has stood as one of the cornerstones of individual liberty and prosperity. It is a fundamental concept that transcends time and culture, enshrining the notion that what one possesses is not merely material wealth but a manifestation of one's labor, dreams, and aspirations. However, the sanctity of property rights has not always been inviolable, and the stories contained within this section, "Betrayed Estates: Property's Conquest by Authority," delve into moments when governments, driven by ambition, necessity, or disregard, have laid claim to the possessions of their citizens. Here, we venture into the realm of property and ownership, where the balance of power teeters on the precipice of betrayal.

34

Eminent Domain

Property - the foundation of individual freedom, a cornerstone of the American dream. Yet, amidst the tapestry of liberty woven into our nation's fabric lies a stark thread of potential betrayal: eminent domain. This chapter ventures into the shadows cast by this power, examining its historical underpinnings, controversial expansions, and the chilling impact it can have on individuals and communities.

A Power Rooted in Ambiguity:

The Fifth Amendment declares: "nor shall private property be taken for public use, without just compensation." This seemingly straightforward statement lays the groundwork for eminent domain, granting governments the power to acquire private property for public endeavors. However, the ambiguity surrounding "public use" ignites the first spark of potential betrayal.

Kelo: Expansion or Erosion?

The 2005 Supreme Court case, Kelo v. City of New London, stands as a pivotal moment. Here, the court's decision expanded the definition of "public use" to encompass economic development, allowing the city to seize private homes for private development, promising increased tax revenue and job creation. This ruling, while upholding the government's authority, ignited fierce debate. Was this a necessary evolution in a changing society, or an erosion of the very property rights enshrined in the Constitution?

Beyond Public Use: The Betrayal of Communities

While intended for public good, eminent domain has often veered into territory far less noble. Communities, particularly marginalized ones, have faced the brunt of its impact. From urban renewal projects displacing residents to land seizures for private corporations, the narrative shifts from progress to betrayal. The question arises: when does public good become a mere pretext for private gain, stripping individuals of their homes and livelihoods?

Just Compensation: A Hollow Promise?

The principle of "just compensation" aims to mitigate the pain of losing property through fair market value. However, this too, becomes a battleground. Property owners often challenge the adequacy of compensation, arguing it fails to capture the true value of their homes, businesses, and the emotional upheaval caused by displacement. This raises doubts: is "just compensation" truly just, or does it leave a residue of bitterness, a sense of being undervalued and unheard?

Navigating the Tightrope: Upholding Justice, Preserving Liberty

Eminent domain remains a necessary tool for infrastructure development and public projects. However, its history is riddled with instances where the scales tipped, where the public good became an excuse for private gain, and where individual rights were sacrificed in the name of progress. Moving forward, navigating this power demands vigilance. Stricter definitions of "public use," robust community engagement, and ensuring truly "just compensation" are crucial steps in preventing this tool from becoming an instrument of betrayal.

Remember, John Adams' words: "The moment the idea is admitted into society that property is not as sacred as the laws of God, and that there is not a force of law and public justice to protect it, anarchy and tyranny commence." As we delve deeper into "Betrayed Estates," let us remember this warning, upholding the sacred nature of property and ensuring that eminent domain serves the public good, not private interests, safeguarding the cornerstone of liberty in the face of potential betrayal.

35

Inflation

While often understood as an economic phenomenon, inflation's impact extends far beyond just numbers on a chart. It carries significant implications for fundamental rights, particularly the concept of property ownership. This chapter explores the nuanced relationship between inflation and property rights, focusing on how government policies can potentially lead to an erosion of individual wealth and challenge the principles of ownership.

Understanding the Mechanism: How Inflation Impacts Currency Value

Inflation, defined as a sustained increase in the general price level over time, reduces the purchasing power of money. Each unit of currency buys fewer goods and services as prices rise. This seemingly subtle shift has real consequences for property rights, primarily by devaluing the real value of individuals' monetary assets. Imagine a savings account: while the nominal value might remain the same, inflation slowly diminishes its true buying power, effectively reducing the wealth stored within.

Government Influence: The Role of Monetary Policy

Central banks, acting on behalf of governments, hold the unique power to manage the money supply through various tools like quantitative easing or interest rate adjustments. These tools, intended to stimulate economic growth or stabilize markets, can inadvertently create inflationary pressures. When the money supply outpaces the production of goods and services, competition for those resources drives up prices, ultimately leading to inflation.

Real-World Impact: Savings, Wealth, and the Erosion of Value

For individuals who rely on savings, inflation acts as a silent thief. The purchasing power of their hard-earned money dwindles with each passing year, eroding their wealth and ability to secure future needs. Retirees, individuals on fixed incomes, and others relying on past savings are particularly vulnerable. Their limited income streams struggle to keep pace with rising costs, compromising their living standards and jeopardizing their financial security.

Lessons from History: When Inflation Becomes Extreme

Extreme cases of hyperinflation, like those witnessed in Weimar Germany or Zimbabwe, serve as stark reminders of the potentially devastating consequences of unchecked inflation. In these instances, the currency became practically worthless, wiping out the wealth and savings of entire populations. These historical examples offer a cautionary tale, highlighting the potential for inflation to violate property rights on a massive scale.

Inflation as a Hidden Tax: Ethical Concerns and Transparency

Inflation can be viewed as a form of indirect taxation imposed by the government. While not explicitly legislated, the effect is similar – a reduction in the value of people's money. This "tax" often remains hidden, lacking transparency and democratic accountability. It raises ethical concerns, as the government essentially devalues its citizens' wealth without their direct consent. This action challenges the very notion of fair ownership and raises questions about the government's role in safeguarding property rights.

Finding Balance: Navigating the Challenge of Inflation

Recognizing the link between inflation and property rights is crucial for navigating this complex issue. Finding a solution requires balancing competing needs: stimulating economic growth without sacrificing the value of individuals' assets. Implementing responsible monetary policies alongside measures to protect against excessive inflation is paramount. Open dialogue and responsible decision-making are essential to ensure that government actions maintain and uphold the fundamental principles of property ownership.

36

Gun Control Laws

The Second Amendment to the United States Constitution asserts, "the right of the people to keep and bear Arms, shall not be infringed." This chapter presents the argument that gun control laws, by their very nature, represent infringements on this constitutionally guaranteed right. It examines the effectiveness of these laws in crime prevention and their impact on lawful gun ownership.

The Constitutional Perspective

The Second Amendment's unequivocal language has been a cornerstone for gun rights advocates. They argue that any form of gun control legislation, irrespective of intent, infringes upon this fundamental right. From this viewpoint, the right to bear arms is an inalienable and individual right, immune to the regulatory whims of legislative bodies.

The Ineffectiveness of Gun Control Laws in Crime Reduction

Since the early 20th century, a multitude of gun control laws has been enacted at both federal and state levels. However, evidence suggests these laws have had no significant impact on reducing crime rates. Studies and statistical analyses often fail to show a direct correlation between stringent gun control measures and a decrease in crime. In fact, some areas with the strictest gun laws continue to experience high rates of gun violence, indicating that factors other than gun legislation play a more significant role in crime dynamics.

The Real Impact of Gun Control Laws

Gun control laws have primarily served to make firearms more expensive and acquisition more challenging for law-abiding citizens. These regulations often involve extensive background checks, waiting periods, and additional financial burdens, which do not deter criminals but do impact ordinary citizens exercising their Second Amendment rights. The cumulative effect is a regulatory environment that restricts access to firearms for self-defense, sport, and other legal purposes.

Historical Context and Legislative Overreach

The history of gun control in the United States is marked by a gradual but steady encroachment on gun rights. Beginning with the National Firearms Act of 1934 to the present day, each legislative act, while often well-intentioned, has incrementally restricted gun ownership. Critics of these laws argue that such legislative overreach not only violates the Second Amendment but also fails to address the root causes of gun violence, such as socio-economic factors and mental health issues.

Case Studies and Comparative Analysis

By examining specific cases and comparing regions with varying levels of gun control, it becomes apparent that these laws have not achieved their intended goals. For instance, cities like Chicago, with some of the most stringent gun laws, have not seen a commensurate decrease in gun violence. In contrast, areas with more relaxed gun laws do not necessarily experience higher crime rates, further challenging the effectiveness of gun control measures.

The Cultural and Social Aspect

The gun control debate is deeply intertwined with the cultural and social fabric of the United States. Firearms are seen by many as a symbol of liberty and self-reliance, aspects that are deeply embedded in the American psyche. Gun control laws are often perceived as not only an infringement on constitutional rights but also an attack on these cultural values.

Conclusion

In conclusion, the myriad of gun control laws enacted over the past century have predominantly served to restrict the con- stitutionally protected rights of law-abiding citizens without producing a significant impact on crime reduction.

37

Zoning and Land Use Regulations

The intricate web of land use and zoning regulations stands in stark contrast to the bedrock principles upon which America was built. The Framers, deeply influenced by Lockean philosophy, enshrined the right to private property as a cornerstone of a just and free society. This right, they believed, was not a mere concession from the state, but an inherent and natural right pre-existing any government.

Euclid v. Ambler: A Departure from the Original Intent?

The 1926 Supreme Court decision in Euclid v. Ambler Realty Co., while establishing the legal framework for zoning, marked a potential deviation from the original intent. While promoting public welfare is a legitimate government function, it must not come at the expense of individual rights secured by the Constitution. The Framers never envisioned a government with unfettered power to dictate land use, a power that could easily morph into a tool for controlling citizens and their economic pursuits.

Zoning and the Erosion of Property Rights:

Modern zoning regulations, often exceeding the narrow scope envisioned in Euclid, pose a clear and present danger to property rights. Restrictive zoning, particularly for small landowners, effectively diminishes the value of their property, depriving them of the full benefit of ownership. This stands in direct conflict with the original understanding of property rights, where individuals held absolute dominion over their land, subject only to minimal, clearly defined government regulations.

Regulatory Takings: A Violation of Just Compensation?

The concept of "regulatory taking" further underscores the potential for government overreach. When zoning regulations render land unusable for its intended purpose, effectively "taking" its economic value, the Fifth Amendment's guarantee of just compensation comes into play. However, modern interpretations often dilute this protection, leaving property owners with little recourse against government encroachment.

Limited Government and the Path Forward:

Navigating the complex landscape of land use regulations demands a return to the core principles of limited government. Zoning authority, if deemed necessary at all, should be strictly confined to its original intent – preventing nuisances and ensuring public health and safety. Excessive regulations, driven by nebulous notions of "public welfare," should be scrutinized with a skeptical eye, ensuring they truly serve a legitimate government function and do not infringe upon individual property rights.

38

Regulatory Takings

The concept of regulatory takings presents a significant challenge in the realm of property rights, standing at the intersection of government regulation and individual liberty. This chapter delves into this complex issue, exploring how government actions, under the guise of regulation, can impinge upon the fundamental property rights that have been a cornerstone of American values since the nation's founding.

Historical Context

The concept of regulatory takings was highlighted in the landmark 1922 Supreme Court case, Pennsylvania Coal Co. v. Mahon. This case set a precedent in property rights jurisprudence, introducing the "harmful or noxious" rule by Justice Oliver Wendell Holmes Jr. This rule laid the foundation for understanding the limits of government authority in regulating property, balancing property rights against the government's duty to prevent activities deemed harmful to society.

The Fifth Amendment and Property Rights

The Takings Clause of the Fifth Amendment, stating "nor shall private property be taken for public use, without just compensation," underscores the constitutional commitment to protecting property rights. It ensures that the government cannot deprive individuals of their property without following due process and providing fair compensation.

Landmark Cases in Regulatory Takings

- **Penn Central Transportation Co. v. City of New York (1978):** This case established the "ad hoc" analysis for regulatory takings, considering the economic impact, investment-backed expectations, and the character of government actions.
- **Lucas v. South Carolina Coastal Council (1992):** This case introduced the concept of "total takings," stating that regulations that deprive property owners of all economically beneficial uses constitute a taking that requires compensation.

Contemporary Challenges and Examples

- **California Coastal Commission:** This commission has faced several claims of regulatory takings due to its strict regulations on coastal property development. Property owners argue that these regulations limit their ability to use and develop their land, leading to significant economic losses.

- **Wetlands Regulations:** The Clean Water Act's regulations on wetlands have sparked disputes over regulatory takings. Landowners contend that these rules severely restrict land use, drastically diminishing their property's value.

Balancing Public Welfare and Property Rights

The challenge in regulatory takings lies in balancing the need for government regulations, which are essential for public welfare, environmental protection, and safety, with the preservation of individual property rights. This balance is critical in ensuring that while public interests are served, individual rights are not unduly compromised.

Conclusion

The journey through the complex issue of regulatory takings highlights the ongoing struggle between government power and individual liberty. Ensuring that government regulations do not overstep and infringe upon property rights requires a delicate balance, one that respects both the common good and the sanctity of personal property. As "Trust Shattered" continues, it will further explore the dynamic and often contentious interactions between government actions and individual freedoms.

39

Property Tax

The concept of perpetual property taxation, where individuals are continuously taxed on assets they already own, raises serious ethical concerns. This practice, deeply embedded in the tax system, particularly with respect to real estate, stands in stark contrast to the principles of fair ownership and economic justice. This chapter argues that perpetual property taxation is not only unethical but also fundamentally flawed, as it leads to scenarios where the cumulative tax burden over time can far exceed the actual value of the property.

Ethical Implications of Perpetual Property Taxation

The core ethical issue with perpetual property taxation lies in its contradiction of the basic tenets of ownership. True ownership implies a degree of permanence and security, where once an asset is purchased, it belongs to the owner free and clear. However, perpetual taxation undermines this security, effectively rendering property ownership a form of long-term rental from the state. This undermines the value of working towards and acquiring property, a key element of the American dream.

Financial Burden Exceeding Property Value

A critical flaw in the system of perpetual property taxation is the potential for the total taxes paid over time to surpass the property's actual worth. This situation is particularly acute in areas with high property tax rates or rapidly increasing assessments. Property owners, especially those on fixed incomes such as retirees, find themselves paying ever-increasing taxes, often on properties that have been fully paid for. The cumulative effect over decades can lead to a situation where the total tax paid is disproportionate to the property's value, questioning the fairness and sustainability of such a system.

Impact on Homeownership and Economic Inequality

Perpetual property taxation has significant implications for homeownership and economic inequality. It disproportionately affects lower and middle-income families, for whom the tax burden can represent a significant portion of their income. This can lead to a situation where owning a home becomes increasingly unaffordable, exacerbating the wealth gap and undermining the ideal of equitable property ownership. Moreover, the burden of high property taxes can force individuals, especially the elderly, to sell their homes, undermining the stability and continuity that property ownership is supposed to provide.

The Cumulative Tax Burden

Examining specific instances highlights the issue more starkly. In some regions, property owners have found themselves paying two to three times the value of their property in taxes over a prolonged period. These cases starkly illustrate how perpetual property taxation can become an unsustainable financial burden, essentially penalizing long-term property ownership.

Constitutional and Legal Considerations

There are also constitutional and legal considerations. The practice of perpetual property taxation raises questions about its alignment with constitutional principles, especially regarding the right to private property. Does this form of taxation infringe upon the constitutional guarantees that protect citizens from unfair and excessive government expropriation?

Rethinking the Property Tax System

In conclusion, the ethics and financial implications of perpetual property taxation necessitate a serious reevaluation of this system. It is crucial to consider alternative models of taxation that are more equitable, fair, and aligned with the principles of true property ownership. Such reforms would ensure that property taxes serve their intended purpose of funding essential public services without undermining the fundamental rights and financial stability of property owners. As we move forward, it is imperative to strike a balance that respects both the needs of the community and the rights of individual property owners.

40

Rent Control

The implementation of rent control policies across various cities in the United States represents a complex intersection of housing affordability concerns and the protection of property rights. This chapter delves into the contentious nature of rent control, analyzing its impact on both tenants seeking affordable housing and property owners whose rights and economic interests are at stake.

The Dual Nature of Rent Control

Rent control policies were primarily introduced as a response to housing crises, aiming to protect tenants from sudden, unaffordable rent increases. These policies cap the amount landlords can charge for rentals, ostensibly providing stability and security for low-income and vulnerable tenants.

However, the implications of rent control extend far beyond tenant protection. For property owners, these regulations often mean a significant limitation on their ability to derive fair market value from their investments. This restriction can discourage maintenance and improvement of properties, leading to a decline in the quality of housing over time.

Historical Context and Rationale

The origins of rent control in the U.S. can be traced back to periods of acute housing shortages, such as during World War II, when it was deemed necessary to protect citizens from exploitative rent hikes. Cities like New York adopted rent control as a temporary measure, which then evolved into a long-term policy. This historical backdrop provides a context for understanding the intentions behind rent control, though it also highlights the evolution of these policies into more permanent fixtures.

The Legal and Economic Debates

Legally, rent control presents a challenge to the concept of private property rights enshrined in the Constitution. The restriction on how property owners can use and profit from their property has led to numerous legal battles, questioning the balance between public good and individual rights.

Economically, rent control is often criticized for distorting the housing market. By artificially suppressing rent prices, it can lead to a decrease in the supply of rental properties. Landlords may be disincentivized to maintain or improve their properties, or they may convert rental properties to other, more profitable uses. This can exacerbate the very housing shortages that rent control aims to mitigate.

The Impact of Rent Control

In cities with long-standing rent control laws, such as San Francisco and New York, the effects have been significant. Studies have shown that rent control can lead to a decrease in the availability of affordable housing, as landlords find ways to circumvent these regulations, often leading to gentrification and displacement of lower-income residents.

Conversely, tenants in rent-controlled apartments often benefit from stabilized rent and increased security. However, these benefits are typically unevenly distributed and do not address the broader issues of housing affordability and availability.

The Argument Against Rent Control

The ethical argument against rent control centers on the infringement of property rights. It posits that property owners should be free to set rents based on market conditions. Government intervention in this process is seen as an overreach, violating the principle of economic freedom and the rights of property owners.

Moreover, the unintended consequences of rent control, including the deterioration of housing quality and the reduction in the housing stock, suggest that it may be an ineffective and counterproductive policy in addressing housing affordability issues.

Seeking Equitable Solutions

In conclusion, rent control presents a complex challenge, balancing the need for affordable housing with the protection of property rights. While its intentions are often noble, the practical implications for both tenants and landlords suggest a need for more nuanced and equitable solutions. Alternative approaches to address housing affordability might involve incentivizing the development of affordable housing, providing direct assistance to those in need, or implementing tax policies that encourage landlords to maintain and improve rental properties without compromising on rent affordability.

These solutions aim to address the root causes of the housing crisis rather than merely treating its symptoms through rent control. They seek to foster a more sustainable and equitable housing market, where the rights and interests of both tenants and property owners are respected and protected.

Balancing Interests in a Dynamic Market

The key to resolving the tension between rent control and property rights lies in understanding and balancing the diverse interests and needs within the housing market. This includes acknowledging the rights of property owners to earn a fair return on their investments, as well as recognizing the basic human need for affordable and stable housing.

Policy Reform and Future Considerations

As urban centers continue to grow and evolve, the debate around rent control and its implications for property rights will remain a crucial policy issue. Future reforms should focus on creating a housing market that is both dynamic and responsive to the needs of all stakeholders. This requires a collaborative approach involving government, property owners, tenants, and urban planners to create policies that are fair, sustainable, and conducive to the overall health of the housing market.

Concluding Reflections

The discourse on rent control and property rights is emblematic of the broader challenges in balancing individual rights with collective welfare. It underscores the need for thoughtful, informed policymaking that considers the long-term implications of such measures on society as a whole. As we continue to navigate these complex issues, it is crucial that we strive for solutions that uphold the principles of liberty, fairness, and economic justice.

41

Environmental Regulations

Since its inception in 1970, the Environmental Protection Agency (EPA) has been tasked with the monumental responsibility of safeguarding the environment and ensuring the health and well-being of the American populace. While its efforts have undoubtedly contributed to cleaner air and water, the EPA's regulatory reach has also extended into the realm of property rights, raising concerns among property owners and constitutional scholars alike.

The Regulatory Tangent

EPA regulations, often born out of noble intentions to protect the environment, can inadvertently impinge upon the rights of property owners, limiting their ability to utilize and develop their land as they see fit. These regulations span a wide spectrum, encompassing everything from wetland preservation to emission standards, all of which can impose significant burdens on property owners.

Example 1: Wetland Preservation and Property Rights

The EPA's Clean Water Act (CWA) mandates the protection of wetlands, areas where water covers the soil surface for extended periods. While wetlands play a vital role in filtering pollutants and providing habitat for diverse wildlife, the CWA's stringent regulations can severely restrict the activities property owners can undertake on their land.

Consider a scenario where a property owner intends to develop a portion of their land for commercial purposes. However, upon closer inspection, they discover that a significant portion of their property falls under the CWA's wetland designation. As a result, their development plans are abruptly halted, and they are forced to navigate a complex regulatory process to obtain permits and comply with the CWA's requirements.

Example 2: Emission Standards and Property Rights

The EPA's Clean Air Act (CAA) aims to reduce air pollution by establishing emission standards for various industries and sources. While these standards may be essential for safeguarding public health, they can also pose challenges for property owners, particularly those operating businesses or industries that emit pollutants.

Imagine a property owner who owns a small manufacturing facility. Their operations fall under the CAA's regulatory umbrella, requiring them to implement costly emission control technologies or make significant operational changes to comply with the established standards. These expenses can strain their financial resources and limit their ability to invest in growth or improvements.

Example 3: Endangered Species Act and Property Rights

The Endangered Species Act (ESA) aims to protect endangered and threatened species by designating critical habitats for their preservation. While the ESA's objectives are commendable, its implementation can have a profound impact on property rights.

Consider a property owner who discovers that their land harbors a critical habitat for an endangered species. Their development plans are now subject to stringent restrictions imposed by the ESA, potentially prohibiting them from altering the habitat or requiring them to obtain special permits. This can significantly reduce the value of their property and hinder their ability to utilize their land as they deem fit.

The Balancing Act: Environmental Protection and Property Rights

While intended to protect the environment, the EPA's regulations must be carefully examined to ensure they do not infringe upon the fundamental rights of property owners. Striking a balance between environmental stewardship and individual liberty is paramount to preserving our planet's health and the rights enshrined in our Constitution.

Protecting the Environment without Sacrificing Liberty

The EPA's role in safeguarding the environment is undeniable. However, its regulatory reach must not encroach upon the fundamental rights of property owners. By prioritizing individual liberty and empowering communities to take ownership of environmental stewardship, we can achieve a more sustainable and prosperous future without sacrificing the principles upon which our nation was founded.

<h1 style="text-align:center">42</h1>

Civil Asset Forfeiture

Civil asset forfeiture without a conviction represents a critical challenge to the principles of property rights and due process enshrined in the United States Constitution. This practice allows law enforcement agencies to seize assets from individuals without the need for a criminal conviction, or in some cases, even charges being filed. This chapter delves into the implications of such a policy and argues that it is not only unethical but unconstitutional, infringing upon the rights guaranteed under the Fifth and Fourteenth Amendments.

Violation of Constitutional Rights

The Fifth Amendment to the U.S. Constitution states that no person shall be "deprived of life, liberty, or property, without due process of law." Civil asset forfeiture sidesteps this fundamental right by allowing the government to confiscate property without the standard of proof required for a criminal conviction. This practice effectively punishes individuals without the due process of a trial, undermining the foundational principle of "innocent until proven guilty."

Moreover, the Fourteenth Amendment guarantees equal protection under the law, yet civil asset forfeiture disproportionately impacts marginalized and economically disadvantaged communities, who may lack the resources to legally challenge the seizures.

Ethical Concerns and Government Overreach

The ethics of seizing assets without a conviction are deeply troubling. This practice places the burden of proof on the property owner, forcing them to demonstrate the innocence of their assets. It reverses the traditional burden of proof in the criminal justice system and places an undue burden on citizens to defend their property rights.

Additionally, civil asset forfeiture creates a perverse incentive for law enforcement agencies. With departments often able to keep a portion or all of the proceeds from forfeited assets, there is a financial motivation to seize property, leading to potential abuses of power and conflicts of interest.

Highlighting the Issue

Numerous cases illustrate the problematic nature of civil asset forfeiture. For instance, instances where individuals have had large sums of cash confiscated during traffic stops, despite no evidence of criminal activity, showcase the arbitrary nature of this practice. These cases often involve individuals who are carrying cash for legitimate purposes, such as purchasing a car or carrying business earnings, yet find themselves unfairly targeted and deprived of their assets.

The Need for Reform

The issues surrounding civil asset forfeiture have prompted calls for legislative reform. Reform efforts focus on increasing transparency, ensuring proper oversight, and most importantly, requiring a criminal conviction before assets can be seized. This change would align the practice with constitutional principles and protect citizens from unjust governmental overreach.

Restoring Trust and Upholding Liberty

In conclusion, civil asset forfeiture without a conviction is a practice that needs urgent reevaluation. It challenges the very core of American constitutional principles, including property rights and due process. By addressing this issue, we can take a significant step towards restoring trust in the justice system and upholding the liberty and rights of all citizens. The preservation of these rights is not just a legal necessity but a moral imperative to ensure justice and fairness in our society.

43

Income Tax

Income taxation, a fiscal mechanism imposed upon the earnings of both individuals and entities, stands as a direct affront to the sanctity of property rights, embodying a government's claim over a portion of one's laboriously earned income. This narrative seeks to dissect the genesis of income tax, its ideological linkage to collectivist tenets, and its contravention of constitutional axioms, framing these elements as a profound betrayal of property rights.

At its core, income tax serves as a governmental tool to amass revenue, extracting wealth from the populace and businesses alike. Yet, this extraction infringes upon the bedrock of a liberated society: the right to own and manage one's assets, inclusive of the labor's yield. Through the levying of income tax, the state appropriates a slice of an individual's holdings for its agendas, thereby eroding the foundational property rights bestowed upon them.

Consider John, an industrious soul who amasses $100,000

annually. The imposition of income tax curtails a substantial fragment of his earnings, currently about thirty-five percent. This not only diminishes his property rights but also restricts his autonomy over financial deployment. This encroachment saps John's liberty in resource allocation, infringing upon his dominion over personal assets.

The Communist Roots and Constitutional Discord of Income Tax

Tracing back to its origins, income tax is ideologically anchored in communism, with Karl Marx and Friedrich Engels championing progressive taxation in the Communist Manifesto as a vehicle toward social equity. The stratagem of levying heavier taxes on the affluent to redistribute wealth mirrors the communist credo, sparking apprehensions over individual freedom dilution and governmental dominion expansion.

In a communist regime, where the state monopolizes production means and wealth distribution, progressive income tax exemplifies governmental overreach, manipulating individual property for redistributive aims. Such practices not only assail individual liberty and property rights but also usurp the role of personal decision-making in resource allocation.

Progressive income tax further clashes with the Constitution, notably violating the principle of equality under the law. The Constitution heralds the tenet that all citizens stand equal, devoid of discrimination or partiality. Yet, progressive taxation discriminates based on income, burdening higher earners disproportionately and undermining the constitutional cornerstone of equality.

The enactment of the 16th Amendment in 1913, institution-alizing income tax in the U.S., marked a pivotal deviation from the Founding Fathers' vision of a restrained government safeguarding individual freedoms. This shift towards a more intrusive state apparatus, vested with the authority to claim citizens' earnings, signifies a departure from constitutional originalism, eliciting concerns over liberty erosion and governmental overreach.

The Perils of Progressive Taxation and Envy's Role

Progressive taxation sanctions not only limitless wealth redistribution, eroding individual property rights but also dampens economic dynamism and innovation by penalizing success. The system's inherent bias against wealth creation, propelled by envy, skews societal values, undermining the merit of personal achievement and deterring economic contribution.

In essence, the progressive income tax, especially in its extremist manifestations, epitomizes a betrayal of property rights, intertwining with communist ideologies contrary to constitutional principles. Such a system, predicated on envy and the punitive redistribution of wealth, detracts from the fabric of individual liberty and property rights, calling for a reevaluation of taxation principles in favor of mechanisms that respect personal freedom and foster societal prosperity.

44

Inheritance Tax

Inheritance tax, also known as a "death tax," represents a notable intrusion by the government into the realm of personal property rights and family legacies. This form of taxation, levied on individuals who receive assets from a deceased person's estate, is often viewed as an ethical and possibly constitutional overreach by the state. It raises critical questions about the government's role in the redistribution of personal wealth and the right of individuals to pass on their legacy without undue interference.

Double Taxation and Ethical Concerns

Inheritance tax is frequently criticized as a form of double taxation. The assets being inherited have often already been subjected to various taxes throughout the owner's lifetime, including income tax, property tax, and capital gains tax. The imposition of an additional tax on these same assets upon transfer to heirs seems not only redundant but unjust, penalizing families for the mere act of passing down their rightfully owned property.

State Implementation of Inheritance Tax

While the federal government does not impose an inheritance tax, several states in the U.S. have implemented their own versions of this tax. These state-level taxes further complicate the issue, as they create a patchwork of regulations that can disproportionately affect families based on their geographic location. The variation in tax rates and exemption thresholds across states leads to an uneven distribution of tax burdens, making inheritance tax a matter of geographical luck rather than a uniform policy. This inconsistency raises questions about the fairness and uniformity of tax laws in the country.

The Burden on Family Legacies

Inheritance tax not only represents a financial burden but also an emotional one, particularly for families who have to sell treasured family assets to pay the tax. This can lead to the dismantling of family legacies that have been built over generations, as heirlooms, family homes, and businesses may need to be liquidated to satisfy tax liabilities. This requirement to dismantle family legacies to meet tax obligations can be seen as an infringement on the right to family property and heritage.

Impact on Economic Growth and Investment

Critics argue that inheritance tax discourages savings and investment, hindering economic growth. By diminishing the incentive to accumulate wealth, inheritance tax can have a counterproductive effect on the economy. It disincentivizes individuals from striving for financial success, knowing that a significant portion of their estate will be taxed upon their death.

Challenges to Property Rights and Liberty

The concept of inheritance tax challenges the fundamental principles of property rights and individual liberty. Taxing someone's estate upon their death infringes on the right to dispose of one's property as one wishes. It also contradicts the notion of a free society where individuals are entitled to the fruits of their labor without excessive government interference.

A Question of Fairness and Liberty

In conclusion, the debate over inheritance tax centers on the balance between the government's need for revenue and the protection of individual property rights. While proponents of the tax argue for its role in addressing wealth inequality, its detractors see it as an unethical and potentially unconstitutional infringement on personal liberty and family legacies. As discussions around inheritance tax continue, it is imperative to consider its impact not just on government coffers but on the fundamental rights and freedoms that form the bedrock of a free society.

45

Estate Tax

Following our examination of Inheritance Tax in the previous chapter, where we delved into the state-level implications on the transfer of wealth, this chapter shifts focus to the federal counterpart: the Estate Tax. Often referred to as the "death tax," the Estate Tax is levied on the transfer of the deceased's estate to their heirs, marking a significant point of contention in discussions on government reach and the sanctity of intergenerational wealth transfer.

Historical Overview

Introduced in 1916, the Estate Tax was conceived as a progressive tool aimed at curtailing the concentration of wealth, distinguishing itself from state-level Inheritance Taxes by its federal scope and its direct impact on estate valuation before distribution to heirs. With an initial top marginal rate of 10%, the tax was designed to address the disparities in wealth accumulation, often inherited rather than earned. Over the decades, the Estate Tax has witnessed extensive revisions, experiencing fluctuations in rates and variances in exemption thresholds, reflecting the ongoing debate over its efficacy and fairness.

Estate Tax and Its Effect on Wealth Succession

The imposition of the Estate Tax profoundly influences the landscape of wealth succession, potentially diluting familial assets with each generational transition. The tax burdens estates with a hefty fiscal responsibility that, in numerous instances, necessitates the liquidation of tangible assets— be it family enterprises, agricultural holdings, or ancestral treasures—to fulfill tax obligations. This disruption not only threatens the economic stability of the heirs but also risks the dissolution of family heritage and the severance of continuity in legacy businesses and farms.

The Contentious Estate Tax

The debate surrounding the Estate Tax is polarized, with critics lambasting it as an egregious infringement on the rights of property owners. Detractors argue that taxing assets posthumously, assets that have already been subject to various forms of taxation throughout the owner's lifetime, is inherently unjust. This federal tax is criticized for its detrimental effects on savings, investment, and the broader economic fabric, particularly impacting family-owned entities by placing them at an inherent disadvantage in comparison to their corporate counterparts.

An Affront to Property Rights and Legacy Preservation

At its core, the Estate Tax is perceived as an affront to the time-honored principle of bequeathing one's estate, an act of transferring guardianship of a lifetime's accumulation to the next generation. This federal impositi on starkly contrasts with the state-level Inheritance Taxes discussed previously, yet both serve as poignant reminders of the challenges faced in preserving wealth across generations. The Estate Tax, in particular, is seen as penalizing diligence and success, undermining the endeavor to cultivate and perpetuate family prosperity through successive generations.

Advocacy for Wealth Preservation

In light of the profound implications of the Estate Tax on the right to bequeath property and the overarching goal of safeguarding intergenerational wealth transfer, a critical reevaluation of its role and impact is imperative. Protecting the legacy and rights of individuals to transfer their estate without undue burden is essential for maintaining the continuity of family legacies and supporting the economic principles underpinning the fabric of society. As such, the conversation around both Estate and Inheritance Taxes must continue, with a focus on ensuring fairness, economic stability, and the preservation of heritage for future generations.

46

Consumer Product Bans

The escalating trend of consumer product bans poses a stark challenge to the principles of property rights and individual autonomy. In a society that cherishes limited government intervention and the sanctity of personal freedom, the ramifications of such prohibitions on our ability to choose and exercise control over our belongings warrant a thorough scrutiny. This discussion seeks to shed light on how consumer product bans represent a profound betrayal of property rights, emphasizing the urgency to safeguard our freedom of choice.

The Essence of Consumer Product Bans

At their core, consumer product bans are regulatory actions that restrict or outright prohibit the sale and use of specific products, under the guise of protecting public health, safety, or the environment. While these goals may seem noble, it's imperative to dissect the deeper implications of these bans on individual rights and liberties. These regulations not only encroach upon our freedom to choose but also signify a governmental overreach that infringes upon our property rights. The narrative that unfolds around "consumer product bans," "product restrictions," and "rights infringement" highlights a concerning trend toward diminishing personal liberties in the name of collective welfare.

The Impact on Property Rights and Individual Autonomy

Consumer product bans directly assault the foundational principle of property rights - the right to own, use, and dispose of one's property as one sees fit. By dictating which products are permissible, the government oversteps its bounds, transforming from a protector of rights to an arbitrator of morality and necessity. This overreach not only limits our choice but erodes the very essence of personal autonomy. Take, for instance, the prohibition of incandescent light bulbs aimed at promoting energy efficiency. Despite the environmental rationale, such bans deprive individuals of the freedom to select lighting solutions that align with their personal preferences or health needs.

Unintended Consequences

The repercussions of consumer product bans extend beyond the immediate restrictions they impose. They often lead to unintended outcomes such as the emergence of black markets and the proliferation of potentially unsafe alternatives. When the government prohibits access to certain goods, it inadvertently incentivizes individuals to seek these items through illicit channels, exposing them to greater risks. Furthermore, these bans can stifle innovation and creativity, as manufacturers may hesitate to invest in new technologies for fear of future prohibitions.

A Call for Rational Discourse

The debate surrounding consumer product bans is not merely about the products in question but the broader implications for individual freedom and government overreach. Advocates of limited government intervention argue for a marketplace where individuals are free to make their own choices, assuming responsibility for their actions without undue governmental interference. This perspective champions innovation and personal responsibility over paternalistic control.

Preserving Consumer Choice and Upholding Property Rights

In confronting consumer product bans, it's crucial to advocate for policies that respect individual liberties and property rights. Protecting consumer choice means advocating for a market that empowers individuals to make informed decisions, free from governmental overreach. It involves challenging unnecessary restrictions that betray the principles of autonomy and self-determination.

Defending Our Liberties Against Overreach

The imposition of consumer product bans represents a troubling encroachment on our property rights and personal freedoms. As defenders of constitutional values and limited government, it is our duty to scrutinize these bans, understanding their broader implications on our rights and liberties. By fostering a discourse that prioritizes individual choice and minimal intervention, we can safeguard our freedoms and protect the marketplace from undue restrictions. In the face of product bans, our collective response should be one of vigilance and advocacy for the preservation of our fundamental rights.

47

COVID-19 Lockdowns

The COVID-19 pandemic, a global health crisis of unprecedented proportions, led to drastic measures by governments worldwide. Among these were lockdowns and business closures aimed at controlling the virus's spread. While public health was the primary concern, these measures significantly impacted economic activities, leading to a profound debate about the balance between public safety and individual rights, particularly the right to earn a living and property rights.

The Genesis of Lockdowns

As COVID-19 rapidly spread, governments imposed lockdowns, restricting movement and mandating the closure of non-essential businesses. Initially accepted as necessary to prevent overwhelming healthcare systems, these lockdowns quickly became a subject of controversy.

The backbone of the economy, small businesses, and self-employed individuals, were hit hardest by the lockdowns. Mandatory closures meant no income, yet expenses like rent, utilities, and loans continued to accumulate. For many, this was a direct attack on their livelihood and the right to conduct business - a betrayal of their property rights and economic freedom.

Case studies abound, from restaurants and local retailers to service providers like hairdressers and fitness trainers, all forced into an indefinite hiatus. The personal stories of business owners losing their life's work, often with little to no government compensation, highlight a grave overreach.

The Constitutional Debate

The lockdowns sparked a legal and constitutional debate in the United States. The Fifth Amendment states, "nor shall private property be taken for public use, without just compensation." However, the question arose: do mandatory business closures constitute a 'taking'? And if so, is the lack of adequate compensation a violation of this principle?

Legal battles ensued, with business owners suing local and state governments. The inconsistency in defining 'essential' businesses further fueled the controversy, as some saw it as arbitrary and lacking transparency.

Economic Fallout and Unemployment Crisis

The economic consequences were immediate and severe. Unemployment rates skyrocketed, with the U.S. witnessing the highest rates since the Great Depression. The lockdowns, while intended to protect public health, inadvertently initiated an economic health crisis.

The government responded with stimulus packages and unemployment benefits, but for many, this was too little, too late. The economic disparity widened, with the lower-income groups and minorities disproportionately affected.

The Mental Health and Societal Impact

Beyond economics, lockdowns had a profound impact on mental health. The stress of financial insecurity, coupled with isolation and uncertainty, led to increased reports of anxiety, depression, and other mental health issues. This societal impact, a byproduct of the lockdowns, further questioned the government's approach to balancing public health with individual rights.

Long-Term Implications and Lessons Learned

As the world begins to recover, the long-term implications of the lockdowns on the economy and individual liberties are still unfolding. The crisis has prompted a reevaluation of emergency preparedness, the role of government in managing such crises, and the importance of safeguarding individual rights even in emergencies.

The COVID-19 lockdowns, while advantageous from a public health perspective, represented a significant challenge to the principles of property rights and the right to earn a living. As we reflect on the pandemic and its aftermath, it is crucial to analyze these measures critically and ensure that any future responses to crises are balanced, equitable, and respectful of individual liberties and economic freedoms. The lessons learned from this experience are vital in shaping a more resilient and free society.

48

Part III Conclusion

Throughout "Betrayed Estates: Government's Conquest Over Property," we have witnessed the unsettling reality of government encroachment on private property rights, a fundamental pillar of individual liberty and economic prosperity. The various examples of eminent domain abuses, regulatory overreach, and property taxation underscore a disturbing trend: the government's expansion of power often comes at the expense of individual rights and freedoms.

The narratives detailed in this book—from the taking of land through eminent domain to the imposition of burdensome property taxes—illustrate not just the financial losses but also the deeper erosion of personal autonomy and security. These actions, often justified in the name of greater public good or economic development, reveal a tendency towards prioritizing collective or governmental interests over individual property rights.

One of the more insidious aspects of these government actions is their gradual and often unnoticed encroachment. Regulations and laws are implemented incrementally, and their full impact on property rights may only become clear when it is too late for the property owners to effectively resist or challenge the overreach. This gradual erosion of property rights sets dangerous precedents, making it increasingly challenging to reverse the course.

The broader implications of these government actions on property rights are profound. They not only inflict direct harm on individual property owners but also ripple through the economy and society. Secure property rights are essential for fostering investment, innovation, and economic growth. Without the assurance that their property rights will be respected, individuals are less inclined to invest in or improve their property, leading to economic stagnation and decline. Furthermore, the erosion of property rights cultivates an atmosphere of uncertainty and fear, stifling entrepreneurial spirit and innovation.

In conclusion, the exploration in Part III of "Betrayed Estates" serves as a critical reminder of the need for vigilance in protecting property rights. These rights are not merely about ownership and economic interests; they are deeply intertwined with the very essence of liberty and the principles of a just society. When the government oversteps its bounds and infringes upon these rights, it undermines the trust between the state and its citizens and jeopardizes the bedrock of a free, prosperous society.

Therefore, it is crucial for citizens to remain informed and engaged, advocating for policies that respect and uphold property rights. By doing so, we safeguard not just individual assets and investments, but the broader ideals of freedom, justice, and prosperity that define our society. This ongoing vigilance is essential to ensure that the conquests of government over property do not overshadow the rights and liberties that form the core of our constitutional values.

49

Conclusion

As "Trust Shattered" reaches its final pages, we are compelled to reflect on the unsettling reality that the episodes of government betrayal outlined in this book are not speculative theories but well-documented, verifiable instances of overreach and misconduct. Each chapter meticulously chronicles events that are firmly anchored in historical and contemporary records, leaving no room for conspiracy but instead presenting a candid exploration of governmental actions.

The narratives within these chapters unveil a series of actions where the government, in various capacities, has faltered in its duty to protect and uphold the rights and liberties of its citizens. These incidents, ranging from infringement on personal liberties to overreaches in property rights, serve as stark reminders of the potential for governmental power to be misused.

This book, however, only scratches the surface. The unsettling question that lingers is: What don't we know? If history has shown us these instances of betrayal, what current actions of our government might only come to light in the years or decades to come? The prospect is concerning, highlighting the necessity for constant vigilance and scrutiny in our republican society.

"Trust Shattered" is more than a historical account; it's a wake-up call to citizens everywhere. It urges us to remain alert, to question and to demand transparency in every governmental action. The lessons learned from this book should not only inform our understanding of the past but also guide our oversight of the present and future.

In our journey towards a future where governmental transparency and accountability are the norms, "Trust Shattered" stands as a crucial guide. It beckons us to ponder deeply about the actions of our leaders and institutions, to remain inquisitive about the decisions that shape our society, and to be unyielding in our pursuit of truth.

This book implores us to consider not only the known instances of government betrayal but also to be mindful of the unseen. It challenges us to stay informed and engaged, recognizing that what is happening behind the scenes today may only become apparent in the future. Our role as vigilant citizens is essential in ensuring that our government remains a body that truly serves its people and upholds the fundamental tenets of liberty and justice.

The stories of "Trust Shattered" serve as a crucial reminder: the price of liberty is eternal vigilance. As we close this book, let us carry forward its lessons, aware of the past betrayals, alert to the present, and watchful of the future. It is only through our collective efforts to demand accountability and transparency that we can prevent such betrayals from recurring and ensure a government that remains true to the principles upon which it was founded.

Epilogue

The Unseen and the Unceasing Vigilance

As the final words of "Trust Shattered" resonate in our minds, we are not only left with a deeper understanding of the documented betrayals by government authorities but also with an acute awareness of the unseen and unknown. This book serves as both a historical recount and a forward-looking beacon, alerting us to the necessity of perpetual vigilance in safeguarding our liberties.

The incidents detailed in these chapters are not concoctions of conspiracy but well-established facts, each shedding light on a different facet of governmental overreach. Yet, the question that remains ominously unanswered is what remains concealed in the shadows of governmental operations today? What actions are being taken that might only be revealed in hindsight, years or decades from now?

This epilogue is not a conclusion but an ongoing narrative of vigilance. It is a call to action for every citizen to remain alert, inquisitive, and unyielding in the quest for transparency and accountability. The revelations of the past serve as a guide, teaching us to scrutinize the present and anticipate the future with a discerning eye.

"Trust Shattered" is a reminder that our role as citizens extends beyond passive observation. We must engage actively in the democratic process, question the actions of our leaders, and demand evidence-based governance. The protection of our rights and freedoms is an unending responsibility, one that requires our constant participation and attention.

As we step beyond the confines of this book, let us carry its lessons into our daily lives. Let us be the watchful guardians of our own rights and those of others, ensuring that the betrayals of the past do not echo into the future. In this unceasing vigilance lies the strength of our republic and the preservation of our cherished liberties.

Nuremberg Code

"Permissible Medical Experiments."
Trials of War Criminals before the Nuremberg Military
Tribunals

1. The voluntary consent of the human subject is absolutely essential. This means that the person involved should have legal capacity to give consent; should be situated as to be able to exercise free power of choice, without the intervention of any element of force, fraud, deceit, duress, over-reaching, or other ulterior form of constraint or coercion, and should have sufficient knowledge and comprehension of the elements of the subject matter involved as to enable him to make an understanding and enlightened decision. This latter element requires that before the acceptance of an affirmative decision by the experimental subject there should be made known to him the nature, duration, and purpose of the experiment; the method and means by which it is to be conducted; all inconveniences and hazards reasonably to be expected; and the effects upon his health or person which may possibly come from his participation in the experiment.

The duty and responsibility for ascertaining the quality of the consent rests upon each individual who initiates, directs or engages in the experiment. It is a personal duty and responsibility which may not be delegated to another with impunity.

2. The experiment should be such as to yield fruitful results for the good of society, unprocurable by other methods or means of study, and not random and unnecessary in nature.

3. The experiment should be so designed and based on the results of animal experimentation and a knowledge of the natural history of the disease or other problem under study that the anticipated results will justify the performance of the experiment.

4. The experiment should be so conducted as to avoid all unnecessary physical and mental suffering and injury.

5. No experiment should be conducted where there is an a priori reason to believe that death or disabling injury will occur; except, perhaps, in those experiments where the experimental physicians also serve as subjects.

6. The degree of risk to be taken should never exceed that determined by the humanitarian importance of the problem to be solved by the experiment.

7. Proper preparations should be made and adequate facilities provided to protect the experimental subject against even remote possibilities of injury disability or death.

8. The experiment should be conducted only by scientifically qualified persons. The highest degree of skill and care should be required through all stages of the experiment of those who conduct or engage in the experiment.

9. During the course of the experiment the human subject should be at liberty to bring the experiment to an end if he has reached the physical or mental state where continuation of the experiment seems to him to be impossible.

10. During the course of the experiment the scientist in charge must be prepared to terminate the experiment at any stage, if he has probable cause to believe, in the exercise of the good faith, superior skill and careful judgement required by him that a continuation of the experiment is likely to result in injury, disability, or death to the experimental subject.

About the Author

Allow me to introduce Peter Serefine: a U.S. Navy veteran, devoted U.S. Mail carrier, Certified Instructor for the Institute on the Constitution, and a Patriot Academy Constitutional Coach. Peter epitomizes the spirit of service, having served both his country and his community with unwavering dedication.

With a high school education and an essential role as a Pennsylvania State Constable, Peter is deeply rooted in his community. He stands as a representative of the diminishing middle class, carrying the aspirations and concerns of his fellow citizens. It was in the midst of the turbulent political landscape of 2016 that Peter felt a profound calling to be an agent of change. This calling led to the creation of "Progress, Really?," a platform designed to spark critical thinking about the direction of societal and political progress.

However, Peter's impact reaches far beyond this initial endeavor. His insatiable passion for enlightenment inspired the establishment of the Liberty Lighthouse, a beacon of insight for those navigating the intricate landscape of today's world. But Peter wasn't satisfied with merely inspiring through words. He took a step further by creating the online Liberty Lighthouse Classroom, a virtual space where he shares the principles of constitutional governance to empower others on their journey.

Balancing a demanding full-time job, op-ed article writing, and book publishing; all of these remarkable efforts unfold against the backdrop of his residence in a quaint Victorian town in Pennsylvania. Sharing in this incredible journey is Staisha Hancock, Peter's cherished partner, whose unwavering patience beautifully complements his passionate political discussions.

Peter Serefine is the embodiment of dedication, a true advocate for knowledge and change, both within his community and far beyond. His life's work is a testament to the unwavering commitment to the principles he holds dear, and his journey serves as an inspiration to all who seek to make a positive impact in our world.

You can connect with me on:
- https://liberty-lighthouse.com
- https://twitter.com/PSerefine
- https://facebook.com/PSerefine

Also by Peter Serefine

A More Tyrannical King

"In order to successfully fight the ideological war of the 2020s, it's critical to have easily-discussed, yet intellectually deep explanations of our current state. It's even more important to have simple, realistic solutions. A More Tyrannical King provides both and is a must-read for every engaged American—regardless of party—who wants to see the return of a Nation that works."

Phil Bell

Director of External Relations

FreedomWorks

So Simple Even A Politician Can Understand

In **SO SIMPLE EVEN A POLITICAIN CAN UNDERSTAND** Peter puts forth some ideas that would greatly simplify government.Politics does not have to be complicated and convoluted. We The People have to find people willing to put forth simple ideas again. This book is examples of simple ideas that would go a long way to solving some big problems.

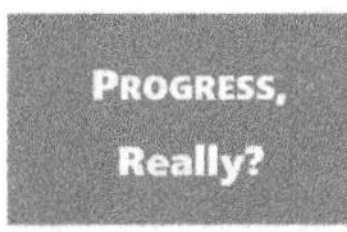

Progress, Really?

"This is a quick read about one perspective on the past, current, and future state of American culture, government, and social standing. The author points out many areas of our country that are straying from its fundamental basis and how continual complacency and acceptance of minority opinions for the sake of appeasing the entitled is quickly leading us toward socialism and an overall destruction of the founding fathers' vision."

Amazon Review

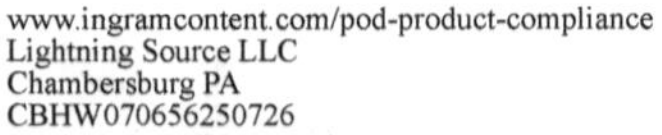
www.ingramcontent.com/pod-product-compliance
Lightning Source LLC
Chambersburg PA
CBHW070656250726

48662CB00001B/152